IT'S TIME

GROW VIGOROUSLY & THRIVE

IT'S TIME

GROW VIGOROUSLY & THRIVE

Life is too short to be miserable.
*Take the test of time and discover a life of
meaning, purpose and fulfillment.*

KRISTI FLOERSCH

© Copyright 2019 by Kristi L. Floersch

All rights reserved. No portion of this book may be reproduced, stored in a retrieval system, or transmitted in any form or by any means – electronic, mechanical, photocopy, recording, scanning, or other – except for brief quotations in critical review or articles, without the prior written permission of the publisher.

Unless otherwise noted, Scripture quotations are taken from The Open Bible® Expanded Edition, Copyright © 1985 by Thomas Nelson, Inc., New American Standard Bible © The Lockman Foundation 1960, 1962, 1963, 1968, 1971, 1972, 1973, 1975, 1977 A corporation not for profit. La Habra, California. All rights reserved.

ISBN 978-1-949950-73-1(e-book)

Library of Congress Control Number: 2019903656
ISBN 978-1-949950-72-4

Printed in the United States of America

To my incredibly talented daughter Alexandra Floersch, who reminds me of my younger self.
May you cherish every moment of time as a precious gift from God, knowing when to slow down when you're going too fast, and when to dive in deep when you have nothing better to do. But most importantly, always listen with your heart.

To download your free copy of the Test of Time visit:
www.flourishnow.net

CONTENTS

Introduction: It's Time to Flourish Now! iii

1. Time is a Choice 1
2. The Choice is Love 7
3. Time is Not Mine 21
4. A Formula for Time to Live 31
5. A Formula for Time to Save 39
6. A Formula for Time to Give 45
7. The Time Tithe 55
8. Time is a Trainer 65
9. You Are Not Alone 73
10. Now Is the Acceptable Time 81
11. Time Is The Period Between Two Eternities 87
12. Planning is a Waste of Time 93
13. Do Not Worry About Tomorrow's Time Today 101

14. A Time For Contentment 107

15. God Is Master Of Time 113

16. The Test Of Time 121

ABOUT THE AUTHOR 142

INTRODUCTION

It's Time to Flourish Now!

Most people either have anxiety about not having enough time to their self, or are depressed about having too much time on their hands. It is a rare commodity to be completely content with the resource of time.

Time is defined as every moment there has ever been or ever will be. A moment is a vague brief period of time. Therefore, the totality of time is made up of infinite moments in a lifetime in which we can be content or dissatisfied based on what we are doing. We have freedom to do what we want. With this freedom comes choice, which is the power to select what to do.

At times in our life, we may have other people who help us make choices of what to do with our time. As kids, parents help us choose what to do as they guide us to make good choices. As students, teachers help us choose what classes to attend and when to attend them.

As we reach adulthood, we are given the sole power to select what to do with our time of twenty four hours in a day. This is where the problem begins. We ask ourselves: "Where have I come from?" "Where am I going?" "Why am I here?" "How can I know the truth?" "How can I make a difference?" "What should I do with my time?" And we not more then begin to ponder the answers to these questions, when a distraction hits us broadside like a train into a parked car on a track and forcibly jolts us in a different direction. The distractions of life steal us away from answering these questions of what matters most. We get so caught up in the distractions around us, that we are no longer able to be fully present in mind, body and spirit.

The answers to the questions motivate us to make good choices of how we spend our time. If we linger long enough and dig deep enough we just might come to understand the unique and beautiful contribution we are here to make. Being present in the moment means to have full control of our feelings and actions. There is a lot to learn about how to use time that results in a life of meaning, purpose and fulfillment.

I suppose in order to write a book about time, I should be an expert. That is not the case. My purpose is not to define time, but rather provide insight on how to use time to grow vigorously and thrive by answering these age old questions. It is a process that will result in a peaceful balance. It is the way that will create a lifetime of joy and contentment no matter what season of life you're in. It will give your life meaning, purpose and fulfillment.

God has given us two resources: time and money. He expects us to be good stewards of these resources, using them to grow His kingdom here on earth at our will. There are three ways in which time and money can be utilized. They can be (1) consumed, (2) saved (or savored) and (3) given away.

Time is much like money, in that I desire a lot of it and never think there is ever enough of it — no matter how much I have. Or, I have much more time than I want… and contemplate what I should do with it. And yet, when I am most fully alive and well, I have just enough time for myself and more than enough time with which to generously and cheerfully serve others.

On one hand, I work, sweat, strive, persevere and press on to my ideal of what to do with very limited time — chasing after it in desperation to own it, if but for a moment. And when that moment arrives, I no more than get a taste of it, and it vanishes. Once again, I sprint after time with sheer determination to bottle it up again. And just when I get a tiny bit of time, I savor it as if it were the most precious thing on earth, attempting to keep it to myself without a thought of sharing it with anyone else.

On the other hand, I often find myself having way too much time, as if it were a never-ending abyss. I simply waste it away in hopes someone will rescue me from it. I mistakenly depend on others to help me escape from the prison walls of too much time. I make other people responsible for helping me do something meaningful with my time. And worse yet, I falsely blame other people if they don't care enough to visit and console me during this time, as if they're responsible for making it valuable for me. I battle the feelings of fear, anxiety, anguish, loneliness, boredom, depression and emptiness from either making poor choices — or no choice at all — with what to do with the time. The truth is that I'm responsible for making the right choice in what to do with the resource of time that God has so graciously granted me.

So the questions about time remain. How do I earn more, buy more, enjoy more, get more or give more time? And what exactly would I do if I had more time? What did God put me on earth to do with my time? Is time mine to have? Or should I simply give it all away? Should my time be prioritized in a certain way? Or should it just be spent without thought? And if I am spending time, am I just expelling it? Should I be savoring it instead? (and if so how?) When I have more time on my hands than I want… what will I do with it? Do I spend it on careless priorities, just waiting for the day to come to an end? Or, do I share my time with a stranger, gambling on faith that it will be valuable and significant for both of us?

Does God have a plan for my time? Is He calling me to make a difference in this world? If He does have a plan for what I'm to do with my time, am I listening and obeying His calling in my life? And, even more, at the end of time, will I appreciate what I did with it? Or will I regret even a moment?

I must admit, throughout the past years I have been plagued by these questions and the mystery of how to best utilize time. And—even at this very moment — I wonder with great anxiety if I will regret what I'm doing with this precious and limited time. Will I use it for good or waste it away on distractions and my own selfish desires and the mistaken belief that I must complete my to-do list? After expending my last drop of time on these petty tasks, will I realize they are endless and eat up as much time as I devote to them?

After careful consideration, prayer and reflection, God has unveiled some answers to these questions, but not to the extent or degree that I can say I am yet satisfied. Nonetheless, I will share them with you. I certainly cannot claim to be a master of time, but I have been given a glimpse — a peep hole — or rather a flash of how God intends for me to use my gift of time. My prayer is that this book will be a blessing and inspiration that helps you discern how you're using time to hear God's calling on your life and take action that results in a lifetime of continuous joy.

Don't wait another minute to grow vigorously and thrive. It's time to flourish now!

CHAPTER ONE

Time is a Choice

God has given us the power of choice. This is the quality that differentiates humans from all other living creatures. My human nature fights the battle every day to make choices on how to use time. I can either make choices according to God's commands or my own selfish desires. The choice is mine.

I make hundreds — if not thousands — of choices in tiny moments throughout each day. If I choose to only please myself in each moment, that pleasure will be just a fleeting memory after having selfishly consumed it. Soon I'll be left with an overwhelming feeling of emptiness. However, if I choose to please God, He will grant me continuous joy that will last longer than I could ever imagine or hope for.

You see, happiness is a momentary fleeting feeling. Joy, on the other hand, is a heart-swelling spiritual realization. It's the realization that an exchange of love has affected both myself and at least one other person and ultimately has caused a ripple effect, progressing and growing to countless other people in some way, shape or form.

When I experience joy, I believe God is pleased with me and is blessing me with His pure love for making the right choice in the moment. To feel joy is to experience God's pure, continuous, unconditional love of completeness, wholeness, and unbrokenness. Joy fills my heart until it's overflowing, instilling the desire to make the next righteous choice of how to spend my time. Is it really that easy to experience a life of joy? If I spend my time making right choices in each moment to please God instead of myself, will I be satisfied?

I believe the answer is yes, but it does not come without a fight on my part. And to that I fight — with all that is in me — to spend time making the right choices to please God and deny my own selfish desires so I may encounter and maintain joy rather than fleeting happiness. That is not to say I can never make a choice to please myself. A life of joy is a life of balance.

I believe God created all things for my enjoyment, and that He values me as His child and desires the best for me. I believe God wants me to pursue the truth of the eternal life He has promised me if only I harness my will to His. This is so I may please Him and enjoy a fulfilled, satisfied, and robust life of peace, joy and abundance by giving my time to grow His kingdom here on earth.

I believe by doing His will, I make right choices to bring others to a closer relationship with His son Jesus who is the way — the truth and the life God has promised for each of us. In the Bible we are told that one name for Jesus is the "Word". This scripture passage is found in John 1:1. *In the beginning was the Word, and the Word was with God, and the Word was God. He was in the beginning with God.* This "Word" (namely Jesus) has much to tell me about how I am to use my time to make right choices. It is through Jesus Christ that I have learned a good many lessons that I practice daily. Jesus said to Thomas in John 14:6. *"I am the way, and the truth and the life; no one comes to the Father, but through Me."* This gives me a hint of how I am to live and spend time making right choices. I believe Jesus is saying if I get to know Him, then I will know the way, the truth and the life. So, I have dedicated a portion of my time each day to dig into the "Word" in order to get to know Jesus on a deeper more intimate level. I am determined and believe that He has all the answers I am in search of.

The Bible is where I find the "Word" of the way, the truth and the life of how to spend time making right choices. I like to think of the word "Bible" as an acronym for B (Basic), I (Instruction), B (Before), L (Leaving), E (Earth). Thinking of the Bible in this respect tells me I have a lot to learn. In fact, at times it seems like an insurmountable mountain of lessons needed to be applied and achieved in a short lifetime, and yet with the "B" meaning Basic, it indicates the Bible is a simple foundation that should be almost second nature to me. I ought to know the instructions so well I could live a life of continuous joy with hardly thinking about it.

But life happens and in a moment I fail to do what I've learned, and I make a wrong choice that makes me sad. When I make the choice to read and study the words in the Bible, I find myself in a kindergarten level of comprehension and ability to learn, even though I have been studying, applying and living its teachings my whole life.

However, this "Basic Instruction Before Leaving Earth" manual has been gifted to me (and you) for my own wellbeing and guide to satisfying the deep desire and longing of my broken heart and soul. It answers the questions of what I should be doing with my time. It tells me what choices I should make to feel joy and experience God's pure, sustained, unconditional love of completeness, wholeness, and unbrokenness. My prayer is that you will come to know the truth of how you are to use your time to make the right choices in this busy world.

Grow Vigorously & Thrive

- If I choose to please God, He will grant me continuous joy that will last longer than I could ever imagine or hope for.
- Joy is a heart-swelling spiritual realization.
- To feel joy is to experience God's pure, continuous, unconditional love of completeness, wholeness, and unbrokenness.
- A life of joy is a life of balance.

CHAPTER TWO

The Choice is Love

We live in a world where time is easily stolen from us by television, radio, internet, movies, social media, digital games, jobs, and other distractions that leave us exhausted, depleted and discouraged with no time to invest in an intimate and personal relationship with Jesus Christ who is Love. But if I make a deliberate choice to say "no" to spending time on the worldly distractions, I free myself up to spend time in the grace and mercy of the unconditional love of Jesus. Oh what joy is the choice of time spent with Love!

Satan or the devil is alive and well on planet earth, equipped with a plan to deceive me and make so much noise in my life that I can't hear God. He will use any worldly device or person to keep me from focusing on the life Jesus died to give me — a life that brings peace, joy, and harmony. How sad it is that I am only one choice away from fulfillment at every moment, and yet I choose to be distracted and depleted. The truth is, God does not intend for me to waste my time on distractions, but instead use my time to get to know Jesus who teaches me how to make choices that fill me up with joy. God wants me to grow vigorously and thrive not become weak and inactive. In order to use my life for good, I must first develop a very intimate and personal relationship with Jesus Christ who is Love.

You may have heard the saying "God is love all the time." Isn't it comforting that no matter what time of the day or night it is, we can turn to God to receive His unconditional love? If someone asks me "Who is God?" my answer is: God is Love.

Jesus tells us in Galatians 5:13-14, *"For you were called to freedom, brethren; only do not turn your freedom into an opportunity for the flesh, but through love serve one another."* To me, freedom is the invitation and privilege of spending time in the presence of God who created me for His enjoyment and for me to enjoy Him and all of His creation. The more time I spend in His presence at every moment of my daily life, the more freedom I earn. To really know God I must use my freedom to spend time studying the Bible and getting to know the almighty character and integrity of Jesus on a very personal level.

Why is it so easy to do what is wrong and so hard to do what is right? God warns me not to use my freedom or my time as an opportunity to lie, cheat, steal or be distracted, but instead spend time developing my relationship with Jesus who is love, and in turn I learn to use my time to love and help others.

Jesus is asked, "Which is the first of all the commandments?" and He replies in Mark 12:30-31 *"You shall love the Lord your God with all your heart, with all your soul, with all your mind, and with all your strength. The second is this: You shall love your neighbor as yourself. There is no other commandment greater than these.*

"These two commandments are called "The Greatest Commandments". The first tells me that I must spend time studying the Bible so that I can truly get to know, comprehend and understand who God is and what He teaches me to have a joy filled life. "You shall love your neighbor as yourself." Jesus is telling me that I am free to make choices, but He also explicitly warns not to turn my freedom into an opportunity for the flesh — the body distinct from the soul. You see, the flesh craves selfish desires. The flesh tempts me to do what feels good, without considering morality — the capability of distinguishing between right and wrong.

The flesh doesn't care about right and wrong, it just wants what feels good, which is a false indicator of the life Jesus wants me to live. In other words Jesus is telling me, don't do what is wrong, just because it makes you feel good. Feelings are fickle, changeable, and unstable. Feelings can promote choices that make us feel good in the moment, but may be detrimental to our future.

We are called or invited to freedom. Meaning, we were given a gift of choice to use for either good or bad. It is our will power, or lack thereof, that enables us to make good or bad choices — or even no choice at all. This will power — the exercise in making choices — can either result in rewards or consequences. This freedom allows me to choose what to do with my time, be it good or bad.

In the second part of the Galatians verse, Jesus makes a turn as to face the opposite direction with the word "but". He says, "... but through love serve one another." Can the truth of how to spend my time really be summed up in that one word ... love? And is the choice of love simply to serve one another?

Jesus tells us the truth when He commands in Mark 12:31 *"You shall love your neighbor as yourself"*. He says you "shall," meaning the choice to do the right thing is to love your neighbor as yourself. He isn't asking us to, He is telling us you "shall" love. It is up to us to obey, or disobey by exercising our will power to make the right choice.

In these simple words, I believe He's saying I am to take time to comprehend, understand, acknowledge, appreciate, and love every other unique, one-of-a-kind person by serving them with the gifts I have been given. I am here to embrace, cherish, and learn from the differences in others instead of accusing, criticizing, judging, gossiping, backstabbing, resenting, and hating those I live and work with every day. Again, why is it so easy to do what is wrong and so hard to do what is right? Well, it can be dependent on how we use our will power to make right choices.

For example when it comes to my health, even though I know that overeating carbohydrates, sweets and fatty foods is not good for me and eating the right amount of fruits and vegetables is good for me, I still make the choice of the prior at times. Why can't it be easier to do what is right and harder to do what is wrong? If I choose to eat fruits and vegetables it makes me feel better and if I eat the carbs, sweets and fatty foods, I feel terrible. So what gives? It's called the will power of human weakness. If I don't exercise my will constantly to make right choices become a habit in what I choose to eat, then I will be stuck in a vicious cycle that finds me gaining weight, losing weight and gaining weight again.

I like to think I always comprehend, understand, acknowledge, appreciate and love people. But in truth, I fail miserably. No matter how high a pedestal I put myself on, if I dig deep enough within, I find the truth is that I fall short and spend too much time exercising my choice of continuing bad habits, instead of breaking them. My choices prompted by will power lead to either rewards or consequences.

In my choice to treat people poorly, it causes a negative reaction in them. The Bible says in Galatians 5:15: *"But if you bite and devour one another, take care lest you be consumed by one another."* I have found this to be an exacting truth. When I choose to treat people poorly, I become consumed by people seeking revenge. In turn they either forcefully defend their opinion, or out rightly attack me in words or actions because of what I did to them. I do not like this truth about myself, but I shouldn't be surprised. Since the beginning of time, man has made choices that went against God's commandments, and therefore created a fallen nature. The choice of the first man (Adam) to go against God's will brought about consequences that demand hard work and sweat all the days of my life just to yield the joy of understanding, acknowledging, appreciating and loving every human being.

Genesis 3:17-19 reads: *"To the man He said: 'Because you listened to your wife and ate from the tree of which I forbidden you to eat, cursed be the ground because of you! In toil shall you eat its yield all the days of your life. Thorns and thistles shall it bring forth to you, as you eat of the plants of the field. By the sweat of your face shall you get bread to eat, until you return to the ground, from which you were taken; for you are dirt, and to dirt you shall return"*.

Because of the problems, noise, and distractions of the world we live in, it takes hard work, sweat, diligence, and purposeful intent to make right choices to spend my time loving and serving God and every person I encounter in each moment. One of the most difficult commandments God expects of me is to love my enemies.

Jesus said in Matthew 5:44-45, *"But I say to you, love your enemies and pray for those who persecute you in order that you may be sons of your Father who is in heaven; for He causes His sun to* rise on the evil and the good and sends rain on the righteous and the unrighteous."

Love your enemies and pray for those who persecute you? This was a lesson I refused to learn in my early years. It didn't seem fair. It seemed ridiculous to purposely be kind to someone who had hurt me. My fickle feelings deceived me into thinking that momentary hatred felt better than loving.

Then, in a leap of faith, I decided to trust Jesus and obey what He was telling me. And in that moment, I realized that any negative feeling I had toward someone else was only hurting me. That revenge is not a reward of strength that overpowers my enemies. Rather, it's a consequence of my choice to administer the same unloving and hateful treatment I experienced and therefore wields back that which hurt me. This brought me down to the same level as the one who hurt me to begin with. Let's face it, I don't want to be that person.

Hate causes hate and love produces love. It's not until that moment that I take a leap of faith and dig deep within me, I harness my will power and use my freedom to make the right choice to follow Jesus's commandment in Matthew 5:44. *"But I say to you, love your enemies and pray for those who persecute you."*

It seems suddenly the sun shines brightly into my soul, the flood gates of heaven open up and God is able to pour His almighty grace into my heart. He fills my being with an abundance of overflowing divine love that can only come from Him. It is in that very moment that I use my freedom to make the right choice unlocking the secret to love.

It means I must go beyond my fickle feelings of head knowledge to reach that deeper choice of faith from my heart. It's the power to believe that in my own humanity I am too weak to love perfectly, but in God all things are possible. So the secret is to acknowledge my weakness, humble myself, set aside pride, and realize that in my sinfulness, Christ died for me. In my accusing, Jesus allows me freedom from guilt and blame. In my criticizing, Jesus forgives me. In my judging, Jesus approves of me. In my gossiping, Jesus keeps quiet about me. In my backstabbing, Jesus is faithful. In my resenting, Jesus adores me, and in my hating, Jesus loves me.

In return for what Jesus did for me, He says in Mark 12:31; *"You shall love your neighbor as yourself.* "This is something I must do — not out of love for my enemies — out of love for Christ who died for me. He showed me the perfect example of love — to die a bloody, torturous death on a cross to save me from my sinfulness. There are times in my life when I make bad choices. At those times, I don't realize I'm willfully making a choice to seek revenge or hurt others. I think I'm making myself feel better, stronger, or more important. I am not as concerned with what I'm doing to others, as much as what I'm doing for myself. My flesh wants me to fulfill its selfish desire of pride to make me feel good, but feeling good only lasts for a moment. That is, until the consequences of my actions take a turn back toward me in the form of revenge and hurtful pangs.

Bad choices caused by momentary feelings bring me increased pain when others lash back. For example, this happens when I gossip about others. Just the other day at work, I spoke negatively about my co-worker. I noticed she had been on a personal cell phone call for a great length of time during working hours and I said "She is constantly on her phone." making myself feel good as if I was so much better than her. I had no concern for how this comment might hurt her reputation; rather, I was just fulfilling my selfish desire of pride to make me feel good. It wasn't long after that I received a personal call from my daughter who was in need of my advice and the conversation lasted quite a while. While on the phone, the co-worker who I had made the negative remark about caught me and gave me the evil eye. I later found out that the person I had made the comment to had told my co-worker what I had said about her and she was upset — rightly so. I understood why she lashed back at me. I had put myself on a pedestal of pride thinking I was better than her when I gossiped about her. The truth is, I wasn't any better than her and I made a bad choice that caused her to lash back at me.

Hate begets hate. The flesh and the Spirit are in opposition to one another. In my flesh, my natural reaction to those who have hurt me is to condemn, seek revenge, and harbor evil thoughts of harm to that person. However, in my Spirit, when I choose to pray for and love those who have hurt me, I am given a divine freedom and release from guilt, blame, and hurt. When I pray for my enemies, I give God permission to take away my bitterness toward that person. In return, God gives me will power and control over my flesh-centered feelings, and I'm able to release the anger, tension, and anxiety I have for that person to God. At that very moment, my Spirit is flooded with a peace that surpasses understanding, and I receive an abundance of joy that can only come from God.

Love produces love. God is pleased with my choice and releases His divine love into my heart. It swells with the comprehension that in Him all things are possible, if only I harness my will to obey His commandments. And at that very moment, I understand I must forgive my enemies, because God has forgiven me of my sinfulness. If I don't forgive my enemies, it's as if I'm saying that I'm above God and do not need to obey His commandments. As a result, I do not allow this divine process to take place. God is the creator who willed the universe into existence, and I certainly am not above Him in any way. Therefore I choose to submit myself to Him and forgive my enemies.

I have learned to humble myself, swallow my pride, trust God and believe in His truth. I have been set free from the torment of Satan. I am so grateful for the courage God has given me to pray for, love, and forgive my enemies. After all, they are not mine, they are His, and only God has the power to correct others. God gives me will power to correct myself. He does not give me will power to correct or change anyone else. Any time I spend trying to change anyone but myself is in vain. The second I begin to judge to others, I am reminded of what Jesus did for me by dying on the cross for my sinfulness. I humbly point my finger back at myself and wonder how I can make changes to myself to be a better person for Jesus' sake. I understand it will take a lifetime to correct my wrong behaviors so that I may become more like Jesus, but time spent correcting myself is a far greater investment than trying to correct or change someone else.

I also know that Jesus infinitely loves me for exactly who I am at this very moment. I am on a lifetime journey of seeking to become more and more like Jesus with each passing day. I continue to live among broken people and people may hurt me from time to time. But because Jesus is the perfect example in forgiving my sins, I choose to forgive. This is the secret. I am not perfect, but I am loved. In John 3:16, the Bible states *"For God so loved the world that He gave His only begotten son, that whosoever believes in Him shall not die, but have eternal life."*

So, how do I make right choices consistently of how to spend my time praying for, loving, forgiving, and serving others? I exercise my will power by making right choices to obey God's commandments so that I may experience the grandeur of love He has to share with me. This is what I long for. This is what I'm seeking. This is the choice I must fight to make in each moment of my life. The choice is love.

Grow Vigorously & Thrive

- Oh what joy is the choice of time spent with Love!
- Satan will make so much noise in my life that I can't hear God.
- I am only one choice away from fulfillment at every moment.
- God wants me to grow vigorously and thrive not become weak and inactive.
- God is Love.
- Feelings are fickle, changeable, and unstable.
- In my accusing, Jesus allows me freedom from guilt and blame.
- The flesh and the Spirit are in opposition to one another.

CHAPTER 3

CHAPTER THREE

Time is Not Mine

Time is not mine. This is God's world. He made it, and He controls it. My part is to be responsive. Time has been given to me as a gift from God. God expects me to be a good steward of the time He has gifted to me and to be responsive to His requests for my time. He makes reasonable requests, but it is my choice to obey what He is asking me to do. I don't always listen and obey.

There is so much noise and chaos in the world that I often forget to be still and listen for God's voice. It takes deliberate and purposeful will power to listen and act according to what God might have me do with my time. If I do not choose to spend time in His presence, the world engulfs me with its problems and attractions. Soon time can vanish and become meaningless. As I look back at life, I'm reminded of the rebellious nature I chose — one that's kept me from God's perfect will for my time. Somehow in those moments when God was asking me to do His will, I thought I knew better and chose my own way instead of listening and obeying His command. I put myself and my own selfish desire above what He had in store for me. As a result, I put myself in danger with the possibility of regret and lengthened the days separating me from the peace, joy and comfort God had in store for me. And yet, God had given me the power of choice and left it up to me to make those choices.

I wasted good many years in a selfish, rebellious pursuit of what I thought would make me happy or give me joy.

And during those years, I felt very little peace with anything I was doing. I was running a race that left me exhausted, depleted, anxious, and anything but peaceful. This is the consequence I earned by not listening and obeying my heavenly Father. I believe during these rebellious times God was on the sidelines smiling and waiting patiently for me to return to Him again. He was right there next to me, inviting me to make better choices. But, lovingly, He allowed my rebellious nature to be a learning tool, creating a stepping stone in which I could eventually rise to a life of peace and abundant joy.

I needed to learn that time is not mine. It is not my time in regards to accomplishing my to-do list. A to-do list is not God's plan for me, it is *my* plan for *my* time. God's plan is that I be always present to Him to hear His still small voice in each moment. That is not to say I cannot have a to-do list available for when God's still small voice nudges me to go about my ordinary tasks. During that time, the to-do list comes in handy, allowing me to get more done in less time so when God's presence invites me to respond to Him, I have accomplished the tasks at hand and can be readily available to respond to His need.

The problem with a to-do list is that it is never-ending, and if I am not conscientious of my need to listen to God's will, the to-do list may easily consume my life. It just might become the obstacle that keeps me from the life Jesus died for me to have—a life that uses all of my natural talents and abilities in a way that glorifies God.

For example, I love to watercolor paint and was blessed to go to college to develop and refine my skill of holding a paintbrush in such a way it became a natural extension of my right hand. Painting is a natural talent that God gave me and my heart's desire is to spend more time using the gift. However, because of my endless to-do list, I rarely take time to paint. The days, weeks, months and years pass by without saying no to my to-do list, and yes to my heart's desire of painting a beautiful watercolor painting that I can enjoy or give as a gift for someone else to enjoy. Another example is I deeply desire to be available to help my aging parents and yet my never-ending to-do list demands that I get it done before I go visit them and offer my help.

I never know what God will call me to do, so I must always be prepared to be responsive and alert — on lookout for those He needs my help with. I may be called to feed the homeless at the Salvation Army at Thanksgiving or offer a bed to my dad after a dispute with my mom. I might donate extra clothing in the winter to a coworker, or spend time shaving my sister's hair, who lost most of it to cancer. I might visit a stranger in prison to share the message of hope in the Bible.

God has given me eyes to see and ears to hear. It is like being a first responder on a rescue squad, going about day-to-day tasks until the emergency call comes in. It's then that first responders drop their to-do list and rush off to be of service in hopes of arriving in time to save a life from the edge of death. They never know what they might find when they arrive on-scene but they have been prepared for the worst case scenario and face it head on. Whether afraid or not, they have committed themselves to rescue and have a job to do. Sometimes it requires doing that job afraid. But even with fear running through their veins, they go anyway. (It's a great lesson: never let fear stop you from doing what God is calling you to do.) The first responders rush into action with fiery adrenaline pumping, assessing the dangers and damages, diagnosing critical needs, and applying the appropriate medical steps for each unique situation.

I believe this is how God hopes for me to use my time. I may not be a professional first responder on a rescue squad, but nonetheless, I am a first responder to God's "still small voice" (the voice of one's conscience). I can go about my ordinary day-to-day tasks until God's still small voice calls me into service. I need to be prepared to drop everything I'm doing on my to-do list and rush into action in hopes to save a life.

Sometimes it may be something as simple as taking time to really listen when a friend calls and needs a compassionate ear. It can mean taking a few extra minutes to tuck kids into bed with a tender love they deserve even if they made mistakes throughout the day. It might mean taking a nap or going to bed early in order to get adequate rest. It's thanking a spouse for taking out the garbage or praying with them as they contemplate going back to school or changing careers. It might mean visiting parents who struggle with loneliness. It can mean painting a picture with a message of hope as a birthday present or gathering at a friend's house to pray for healing or support through a difficult situation. It might be cheerfully volunteering to be of service in church. It can mean cleaning a neighbor's house in hopes of giving her a minute to herself while raising three small children. It can mean buying groceries for a kid who's moving out on their own for the first time or praying for God to help a son to pass the test he stayed up half the night studying for. It can mean writing an encouraging letter to young men and women who make the hard choice to enlist in military basic training. It can mean being by the side of a dying father-in-law to comfort him as he goes to meet Jesus or calling, visiting and checking in with a widow after the passing of her lifelong spouse. It can mean taking unpaid time off work to support a sister-in-law through a difficult trial or offering a friend a place to stay while separated from her husband. It can mean sharing an inspirational book with someone who's been suffering with depression or volunteering for the Salvation Army to ring the red kettle bell during Christmas. It might be coordinating a golf tournament to help a non-profit raise money for a new facility or even taking a mission trip to a third-world country to dig a well for clean water.

Whatever God's call is, I can do it by listening for His still small voice, assessing the situation, diagnosing the critical need, and applying the appropriate steps for the given situation, whether afraid or not. Because the reality is, time is not mine. It has been gifted to me by God. My role lies in being responsive, serving His people by being alert and prepared. To be prepared means knowing that my to-do list does not take priority over those who are in need. In other words, even though accomplishing things on my to-do list makes me feel good, I must be prepared to set it aside and listen and obey when God's prompting on my heart tells me to go out of my way to bring an inspirational book and pray with a friend recently diagnosed with cancer. This can seem like a daunting, scary request but since God put it on my heart, I must believe that she needs my help and take a leap of faith to follow through with His call.

When I realize time is not mine but rather a present from God, I begin to cherish time as a gift. I begin to hold dear the time my loving, heavenly Father has given me. I begin to realize that the time God has gifted me is intended to be put into service for those I come in contact with. A certain amount of time has been gifted to me to be a good steward of. How much time have I been gifted to make a difference in this world? How many years, months, days or hours do I have left? Only God knows the answer, but I know that my time on earth is limited. I know one day, this precious time on earth will run out. And therefore, I will — with all that is in me — fight to do His will in each moment. In order to do His will, I need to be clear about what He's asking me to do. In order to be clear, I need to spend time with Him. Like any relationship, the way it grows stronger is by spending time in it. Time is God's. He has gifted this resource to me to use as I choose. I choose to share it with Him, because time is not mine.

Grow Vigorously & Thrive

- Time has been given to me as a gift from God.
- God is right there next to me, inviting me to make better choices.
- Never let fear stop you from doing what God is calling you to do.
- I know one day, this precious time on earth will run out.
- Like any relationship, the way it grows stronger is by spending time in it.

IT'S TIME ~ FLOURISH NOW

CHAPTER FOUR

A Formula for Time to Live

Time and money can be utilized in three ways. They can be consumed, saved, and given away. If I look at the lessons God has shared about money and apply those to how I spend my time, I find this formula. Live on 80%; Save 10%; and Give 10%.

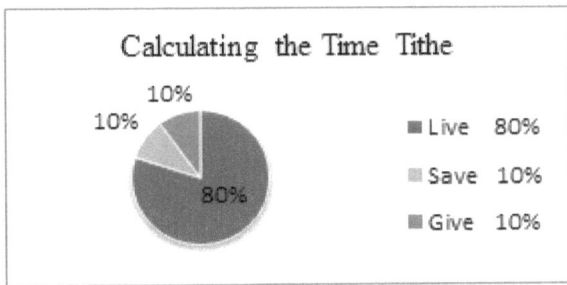

If calculated in real time, using 24 hour day, it looks something like this:

- Live on 19.20 hours.
- Save 2.40 hours.
- Give 2.40 hours.

If you break this down into a day in real life, you can see how it should play out. But in order to do that, first I need to define what it means to Live, Save and Give in terms of time. To Live means to enjoy a full life. To Save means to store up or stockpile, and to Give means to make a gift of. These simple meanings in and of themselves give me instructions on what to do with this resource of time.

The largest sum of time available is that which I live on — 19.20 hours to be exact. If I take a look at some of the basic necessities I need to enjoy a full life (or to Live), I can easily define what I might do with the 19.20 hours. First, I believe in order to live a full life I must get the proper amount of rest so I can be the best version of myself each day. Many studies from the National Sleep Foundation suggest that healthy adults have a sleep need of eight hours each night. That leaves me with 11.20 hours. I have found I truly need eight hours of sleep in order to feel my best and have the most energy each day. It is important to schedule sleep and make it a priority. Having a routine of what time you go to bed and sticking with it is key to making sure you deposit enough time to this important investment.

For example; if you have an iPhone, you can set a bedtime alarm in the clock app that will help you go to bed and wake up at the same time every day to achieve your best rest.

Next, I believe I must consume proper nutrition throughout my day in order to live a healthy life. To prepare a well-balanced meal, I can usually account for about forty minutes. I learned early on that three balanced meals per day — eaten every four hours — keeps me energetic. I have also learned that by eating slowly and without distractions, I savor my dining experience more and am able to stop eating when I am full. According to Webmd.com, it takes approximately 20 minutes from the time you start eating for your brain to send out signals of fullness. Leisurely eating allows ample time to trigger the signal from the brain that you are full. And feeling full translates into eating less. So, in order to stay healthy and prepare and consume the proper nutrition each day, I spend forty minutes preparing and twenty minutes eating which equals one hour — three times per day — equating to three hours.

I believe investing time in preparing healthy meals ultimately gives me time back in the way of not needing to go to the doctor as often because eating and drinking the proper nutrition starves off viruses and strengthens the body to heal it. Let food be your medicine and medicine be your food.

Now, I realize that in busy schedules, this amount of time for preparing food and eating is excessive, and it will vary depending on each day's circumstance. However, for the sake of this example, I will use three hours. So of the 11.20 hours that remained previously, I'm now left with 8.20 hours to live on.

If you think about 11.20 hours, this is the time we spend during the daytime. It is the time we use to make progress, to accomplish something, to enjoy, to work, to play, to live. This time will look different for everyone. But one important thing to consciously assess and ask yourself is; what is my purpose? What am I called to do or to be? How can I make a difference?

For some of us, eight hours of our 24 hour day is spent working at a job to earn money and pay the bills. For others who are enjoying retirement, this same eight hours might be spent doing exactly what you want or feel like doing (or at least it should be). If you aren't enjoying this eight hours, I suggest you take a moment and redesign this time to start doing what you want to do. We are creatures of habit and most find it difficult to quit working to some capacity, but now is your time to do all of the things you've dreamed of doing over the years. So stop and make a deliberate decision on what you want to do with this time and start doing it. Retirement is God's gift of eight hours of time given back to you — time you have earned over your lifetime.

Think hard about what it is you truly, from your very core, love to do. When you were a kid, what are some of the things that really made you happy? What are the experiences you've had that you truly enjoyed? If there wasn't a television, or a smartphone or an internet, what would you do? If money wasn't an obstacle, what would you like to try? If you weren't afraid to try something new and different, what would it be? These are such incredibly important questions to answer. If we don't answer these questions, we fall victim to life controlling us instead of us designing the life we are called to live.

So, after eight hours of work or play, we're left with 10 minutes left to live on. Ten minutes is easily consumed by taking a shower or other things in our daily life. This takes care of the work week, but what will I do to live during the eight extra hours available on the weekend? Usually, for the working population, this time gets filled up fast with necessary tasks around the house. (Think: doing laundry, cleaning the house, paying bills, mowing the lawn, weeding the garden, and the like.) If you ask me, these sound an awful lot like work, too. But, there's also the occasional birthday party, wedding, funeral and other events that fall into this living as well. There in effect is an example of where 80% of time is being lived to the full. To Live means to enjoy a full life.

Grow Vigorously & Thrive

- To Live means to enjoy a full life.
- Schedule eight hours of sleep and make it a priority.
- Consume the proper nutrition in order to live a healthy life.
- Let food be your medicine and medicine be your food.
- Retirement is God's gift of time given back to you.
- Think hard about what truly, from your very core, you love to do.
- Design the life you were called to live.

IT'S TIME ~ FLOURISH NOW

CHAPTER FIVE

A Formula for Time to Save

Next, let's take a look at saving 10% of our day or 2.40 hours. Remember: to save means to store up or stockpile. What this means is to take a couple hours each day to do something that makes me feel truly joyful—something that will give me great pleasure. I believe that God desires me to savor this precious 2.40 hours in my day by doing something I profoundly enjoy. He loves me dearly and wants to lavish and spoil me by giving me this wonderful gift of freedom to myself each day. My responsibility is to set aside 2.40 hours for me alone. He intends for me to receive it gracefully as His gift to me. By accepting this truly needed and life-changing gift from God, He has given me permission to savor something that will make this day a joy. It's hard to explain, but if I give myself permission to enjoy time just for me, it's as though I fill myself up and in turn can thoroughly enjoy the rest of my day and graciously share it with everyone I encounter.

In my earlier years when the kids were little, I didn't take any time for myself, and I can tell you I suffered greatly from anxiety. Even more, everyone around me suffered from my attitude. I was exhausted and depleted. Then, thankfully my sister said something that stopped me in my tracks. I had been getting up to go to work at 5 a.m. during the busy season. I have always stated I am not a morning person. When the busy season was over, I would sleep in until 6:40 a.m. That's when my sister said, "It sure is funny how you can get up early and go to work, but you can't get up early to do something good for yourself!" That hit me square between the eyes. The following week I began setting my alarm to 4:50 a.m. and have been doing so ever since.

One way I savor is spending an hour and forty minutes in my prayer room. It's a tiny bedroom that was once a baby room and later converted into an office. In one corner I have a candle stand with a candle I ignite to represent the light of Christ in the room with me. Beside it is a small lamp with a shade made of tin and punched with holes so the light can escape to create soft patterns in the corner around it. Taped to my candle stand is a photo of my family and a little sign that hangs from an antique knob that says "Leave the rest to God". Above the candle stand hangs a unique cross formed from multi-colored crystal stones that soak in the light from the candle and lamp and reflect it back to me as if it were somehow alive.

And most importantly, above the cross I have a beautiful picture of Jesus.

No matter where I am in the room, He is looking straight into my eyes and reminding me that He loves me so much that He died on the cross to save me from my sinfulness. Here is where and how I love to savor my time as often as possible. On the weekends, I can easily spend a couple hours devoted to prayer and learning Scripture. During the work week, I make 1.40 hours to spend in my prayer room before I need to get ready for work.

But still, that leaves me with another hour to savor. There are many other things I enjoy doing. For example, many days I will spend an hour exercising with a group of women. Other days I like to watercolor paint, read a good book or, in this case, write a book. This is the time I must be most careful not to abuse. Without thinking, it's very easy for this time to be spent or wasted scrolling through social media. I say "wasted" because once that time is spent, I can't get it back and I don't gain the peace as I might have if spent in the presence of God.

Peace is what I long for. The instructions in this book are what it takes to find the peace and freedom we so desperately search for. It would be easy to indulge myself in the selfish things I like to do without care or consideration of the time God has gifted to me. But as I mentioned earlier, I have learned the consequences of going my own selfish way, and it only left me exhausted, depleted, anxious, and far from peaceful. Therefore, I choose to Save 10% of my time — just the right amount of time that sustains me so I can truly enjoy the rest of my life.

Grow Vigorously & Thrive

- Take 2.40 hours each day and do something that makes you truly joyful.
- God intends for me to receive this time gracefully as His gift to me.
- Do something for yourself that you enjoy doing every day.
- Peace is what I long for.
- Leave the rest to God.
- I choose to Save 10% of my time every day.

IT'S TIME ~ FLOURISH NOW

CHAPTER 6

CHAPTER SIX

A Formula for Time to Give

Now that I have spent 21.60 hours of my day, I still have 10% or 2.40 hours to give to others. To Give means to make a gift of my time for the enjoyment or pleasure of others. This is another area of time I have had to learn some hard lessons from. In the past, I used to think of giving my time so as to please people. I was once known as a people pleaser, and rightly so.

Since then I have learned that giving to others means something entirely different than pleasing people. I used to find such incredible satisfaction in pleasing others, that I became addicted to it, as if it were a drug that had an infinite hold on me. I thought I was right in always putting others before myself, until I realized Jesus died on the cross for me and loves me for exactly who I am. The truth of the matter is that the underlying reason for being a people pleaser had more to do with low self-esteem than with doing the right thing.

As I continued down this path of pleasing people, I neglected myself. Eventually I ended up despising pleasing other people because of what it was doing to me. It sucked the life and energy away from me. It made me sick and depressed because I would give so much of myself to please others, but would not get the same attention in return and started to believe that I somehow didn't deserve it and felt worthless. That people didn't care as much about me as I cared about and for them. It was a generalization that was my reality.

People pleasers want everyone around them to be happy and will do almost anything at the cost of their own energy, health and happiness. They have a deep need for approval and are afraid if they say no, people will get mad at them and reject them. So naturally, avoidance of saying no becomes the answer. However, by always saying yes to everyone's request, it steals time away that could otherwise be put towards fulfilling one's self, rather than depleting one's self. But then what is the proper way to give of my time to others? II

A Formula for Time to Give

Corinthians 9:7 says, *"Let each one do just as he has purposed in his heart; not grudgingly or under compulsion; for God loves a cheerful giver."* This passage deals with the attitude one should have in giving — it should be cheerful. When giving is cheerful, it will also be generous. This is such a great measurement tool for me to decide whether or not I should be giving of my time to others. I should give when I feel good about it, and I am cheerful. This makes my heart happy!

Growing up, my tendency was to try to stay out of trouble, because I didn't want to be the one who upset the apple basket, so to speak. I didn't want to be the cause of someone getting mad. So, I found if I always tried to please people — whether it was my mom, dad, siblings, friends, boss, co-workers or the like — then they would like me and my world was round and perfect.

As time passed, I found this was a very juvenile way of thinking. Eventually I learned the more and more I did to please others, the more and more they wanted to take from me and even began demanding time from me, even if I didn't have the desire or energy to give it to them. And if I would say no, ultimately that person would be mad at me, if only temporarily. I used to think that person would never like me again. In fact, I had a friend in grade school that would get mad at me for some silly reason and choose not to speak to me for weeks on end. This happened over and over again, and many times I didn't even know what I did or said to make her mad at me in the first place. I often wondered if she would ever let me be her friend again. Needless to say, this was devastating at such a young, vulnerable age.

After that, I just allowed my feelings to be hurt by countless other people that still at one point or another would get mad at me anyway. Each time I took it personally and thought I wasn't worthy of their friendship. I adopted a worthless mentality — the feeling I was insignificant and unimportant to people. The worthless mentality affected my self-esteem and kept me in the people-pleasing role for years to come. Not until the words Jesus spoke to me and revealed the truth did I change my ways. People-pleasing is something I'm doing for someone else — something I don't necessarily want to do. People pleasing is a one way street that satisfies the other person, but leaves me feeling sacrificed. So, I finally learned the difference between pleasing and giving.

God wants me to give some of my time away as a gift to others. If I'm giving my time to someone, it's in no way a sacrifice. I'm giving it freely. I'm doing it cheerfully from my heart, not in order to please someone. I do it because I want to

A Formula for Time to Give

do it, without expecting anything in return. The funny thing is, when I give my time to someone, my heart automatically overflows with joy, causing me to want to give more. So in giving, I find I also receive. Many times Jesus asks us to give anonymously. In Matthew 6:3-4, Jesus says, *"But when you give alms, do not let your left hand know what your right hand is doing that your alms may be in secret; and your Father who sees in secret will repay you."*

One year during Lent, I chose to smile as much and as often as possible. I conducted a little experiment that would help me understand the impact of giving a smile to not only myself but others around me. (I even tried to fall asleep smiling in the dark.) The amazing thing is that somehow it released a chemical in my brain that made me… well, happy I guess. There were times when I noticed I wasn't smiling, and the alternative was a frown. I lingered while frowning, trying to see how it would make me feel. I quickly noticed my attitude was very hum-drum and seemingly counterproductive, encouraging me to focus on the negative aspects of my life, like how tired I was, the aches and pains in my body, or the mood associated with a cloudy day. However, when I realized I wasn't smiling, I deliberately began to smile on purpose and quickly thought of how good I felt, how beautiful the ray of sunshine was coming through the window, or how nice it was to see rain as it would no doubt make the flowers grow. Not only did I notice the impact smiling had on my own attitude, it seemed as though it was somehow a small gift I was sharing with others who looked at me. They seemed to interact with me more and treated me as a safe haven for sharing stories and personal details.

In earlier years, I was known as the girl who was always smiling. In 9th grade I decided to smile and say hello to everyone I would meet in the hallway. I had no idea that it was making an impact on anyone until I was honored as Homecoming Queen. Even though I didn't know every person personally, they had received the gift of a smile from me which earned their vote. Then, life hit me hard a few times, and that automatic forthcoming smile drifted and faded away with the problems of life. Jesus taught me I don't have to handle my problems by myself. Matthew 11:28-30 says *"Come to Me, all who are weary and heavy-laden, and I will give you rest. Take My yoke upon you, and learn from Me, for I am gentle and humble in heart; and you shall find rest for your souls. For My yoke is easy, and My load is light"*

A Formula for Time to Give

Once I learned to rely on Jesus through all circumstances, I decided I had a lot to smile about. Smiling on purpose has taught me to see things the way Jesus wants me to see them. Smiling has taught me to trust God again and enjoy people and the problems that come with everyday life. I tell you this story, because it's one small way I have chosen to spend part of my 10% of time to give to people. I invite you to join me in smiling for the rest of your life, knowing and trusting that God has a great, unique plan for your life. I know that in giving I shall receive. There are countless ways I can bless others with my time by giving cheerfully from my heart.

Though I've learned a formula for balancing my time is Live on 80%, Save 10% and Give 10%, I would be foolish to think I can schedule my time in exactly this way every day. God has a way of interrupting my best laid plans, to fulfill His purposes in which I gladly obey. However, I want my life to have a balance that glorifies God and helps to grow His kingdom every day. By thinking of spending my time in this way, I purposely decide to choose and commit to seeking out those who hunger for help. As Victor Hugo, a French dramatist, novelist, and poet who lived from 1802 to1885, stated, *"He who every morning plans the transaction of the day and follows out that plan, carries a thread that will guide him through the maze of the most busy life. But where no plan is laid, where the disposal of time is surrendered merely to the chance of incidence, chaos will soon reign."* This is a very exacting truth.

Life without a plan to do good and be good, results in life passing us by. At the end of my life, I want to know that I spent my time doing God's will. I believe God's will is to invest a small portion — 10% — of the precious time He has gifted to me in making someone else's life not only more tolerable, but filled with hope.

Hope comes from getting to know and entering into a personal relationship with Jesus, so that no matter what circumstances and changes affect us, we can still smile knowing we are loved beyond measure by a God who sent His son to die for our sins. This is the message everyone deserves to hear in order to bring about hope in a noisy world. I want to be someone who carries this hope to people in my daily life.

So, this formula for spending time is a guideline to help me align my purpose with the will of God in my life. I realize some days this formula might not always work out the way I plan. But I can make my best effort each day, and if the formula doesn't work some days, I allow the week, month, or year to catch me up in areas I may have fallen behind.

Grow Vigorously & Thrive

- To Give means to make a gift of my time for the enjoyment or pleasure of others.
- Let each one do just as he has purposed in his heart; not grudgingly or under compulsion; for God loves a cheerful giver.
- When giving is cheerful, it will also be generous.
- Smiling on purpose taught me to see things the way Jesus wants me to see them.
- We can smile knowing we are loved beyond measure by a God who sent His son to die for our sins.
- He who every morning plans the transaction of the day and follows out that plan, carries a thread that will guide him through the maze of the most busy life. But where no plan is laid, where the disposal of time is surrendered merely to the chance of incidence, chaos will soon reign.
- Hope comes from getting to know and entering into a personal relationship with Jesus.

- God's will is to invest a small portion—10% of time in making someone else's life not only more tolerable, but filled with hope.

CHAPTER SEVEN

The Time Tithe

The time tithe follows the Biblical formula God gave us in the allotment of what to do with money, using the 80-10-10 rule of tithing. The word tithe means a tenth of one's income paid to a church. Leviticus 27:30-33 says, *"Thus all the tithe of the land, of the seed of the land or of the fruit of the tree, is the Lord's; it is holy to the Lord. If therefore, a man wishes to redeem part of his tithe, he shall add to it one-fifth of it. And for every tenth part of herd or flock, whatever passes under the rod, the tenth one shall be holy to the Lord."* I believe what this verse is saying is if I choose not to give the whole tenth of my income — or in the case of time — which is holy to the Lord, then I will have to pay an additional one-fifth to keep what I already have. No matter what, if I choose to only give part of the one-tenth to the church, it will cost me one-fifth (or 2%) in addition to what I did give. So, if I choose to give only 7%, another 2% of inadvertent cost will be added resulting in 9% of my net income being distributed beyond my control.

In my humanity, I sometimes think I'm smarter than God and looking at my finances, I don't think that I can afford 10% of the tithe, so I skimp. The funny thing is for as long as I have been skimping, I have struggled to pay the bills. My disobedience has resulted in a long and burdensome road of just getting by day to day, not having any extra money or time to give, share, contribute, or enjoy. Not only that, but if I decide to take one-tenth of the tithe and exchange it for something I want instead, then both the original one-tenth and the one-tenth I spend on my own selfish desires shall become holy.

In other words, when I chose to disobediently spend the one-tenth on myself, I also choose to give an additional one-tenth of my income away, resulting in a net loss of 20%. In my humanity, this calculation does not add up because I can run the numbers and legitimately see what I owe. Often what I owe to my mortgage, creditors, and debtors seems more important to spend my money on then the tithe I'm commanded to give by God. In the end, I believe this tithe — this holy calculation—is not mine to understand or be able to calculate because it resides in the spiritual kingdom. This kingdom is the Lord's and everything in it belongs to Him, including time and money.

Romans 11:33 says, *"Oh, the depth of the riches both of the wisdom and knowledge of God! How unsearchable are His judgments and unfathomable His ways! For who has known the mind of the Lord, or who became his counselor? Or who has first given to him that it might be paid back to him again? For from Him and through Him and to Him are all things. To Him be the glory forever. Amen."*

This proves I shouldn't try to calculate it; rather, I must trust and believe the Word and give my tithe to the church in order to have an abundant life and be able to give hope to the less fortunate and vulnerable. Matthew 21:22 states, *"And all things you ask in prayer, believing, you shall receive."* To believe means to take as true or real, or to trust a statement or promise of. I choose to believe the Word of God. Money and time are not mine, though in my humanity, I selfishly guard them as if I know the best way to spend them. It reminds me of my old black Labrador retriever, Chevy. He guarded the house like he knew what was best for me. Even when the UPS truck would deliver a package I had been waiting anxiously for, Chevy would nearly bite the poor driver's leg off before he was able to deliver the important package to me. I think this is how I react with money and time, as if I know better than God in how to use or spend it, when in fact, I bite the very hand that feeds me. I know God created humans to have authority over all living creatures. Genesis 1:26-28 states, *"Then God said, 'Let Us make man in Our image, according to Our likeness; and let them rule over the fish of the sea and over the birds of the sky and over the cattle and over all the earth, and over every creeping thing that creeps on the earth.' And God created man in His own image, in the image of God He created him; male and female He created them. And God blessed them; and God said to them, 'Be fruitful and multiply, and fill the earth, and subdue it; and rule over the fish of the sea and over the birds of the sky and over every living thing that moves on earth."*

With this in mind, I have the power to choose what to do with the time and money God gave me. I am not a dog that cannot control his instincts. In writing this book, I must be obedient to God in giving my time and money. I'm committed to giving my entire tithe. That doesn't mean a portion of it; it means *all* of it. In God's words, I have been created superior over every living thing that moves on earth, and I choose to believe and trust in God's promises. That means if I give 10% of my time to trusting God, He will multiply the time I'm able to give and, in turn, bless me abundantly with time that provides peace, love and enjoyment in my life.

The following is a chart of how time in the allotment of hours equates when spent in a day, a week, a month, a year, five years, and 10 years.

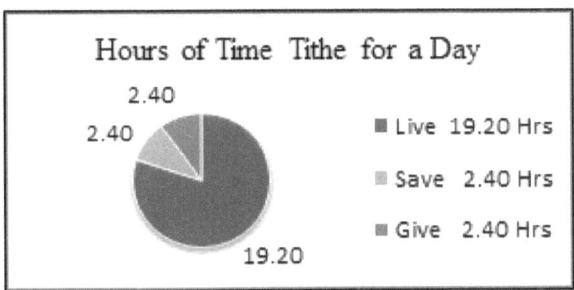

This chart is self-explanatory. It is easy to see how much time to spend in each category per day. In a 24 hour day, Live on 19.20 hours, Save 2.40 hours and Give 2.40 hours.

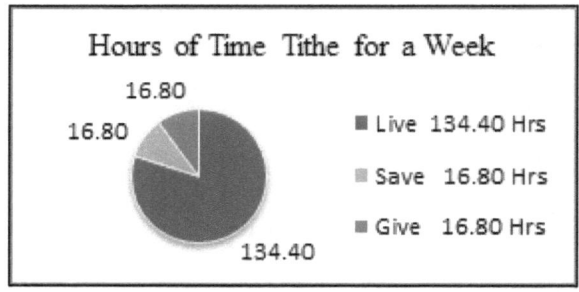

In this chart spanning a week, I begin to recognize hours in terms of days—with 134.40 hours being equivalent to 5.6 days (with 24 hours in a day) to Live on and just over 2 days to Save and to Give.

This third chart corresponds to a month of time (using 30 days). Living on 576 hours is equivalent to 24 days. Saving 72 hours is equivalent to 3 days, as is Giving 72 hours. This puts time into perspective.

The Time Tithe

When I look at time in the allotment of a year, I find I should be living 292 days of the year, and I get to Save 36.50 days to enjoy and Give 36.50 days. From my perspective, that's like getting a raise! For others, it might suggest a little over indulgence of self-saving and may be an area to reassess. It also shows I need to Give 36.5 days of my time—oh my. I know I need to step up to the plate on this one. I haven't tracked time on this in the past, but I'm quite certain I fall short. How does giving 36.5 days of a year to someone else make you feel?

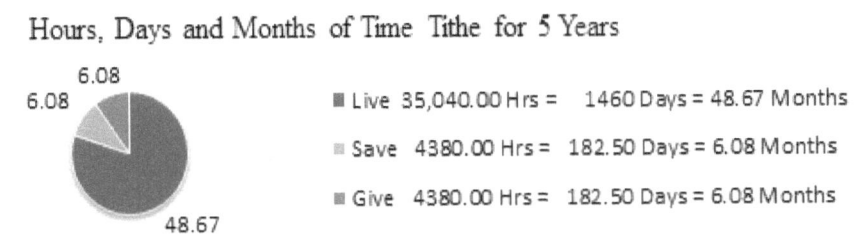

This chart blows me away because it shows I must live on 48.67 months, or four years, in a five-year span. But that isn't what gets me. It's the idea that one whole year of my life is spent Saving and Giving my time to others. I don't know about you but, for me, five years flies by pretty fast. Looking back on the last five years, I can't calculate where I spent six months saving time for myself, or giving six months of my time to others. This chart reminds me of dieting: just when I think I'm doing really good, I get on the scale and realize I wasn't as disciplined as I should have been.

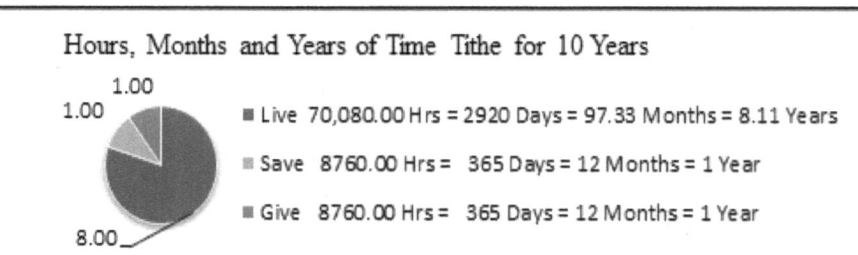

Here again is another eye opener. Out of a ten-year length of time, if I want to live a fulfilled life with abundant joy and peace, I must Live on 8 years, Save one year for myself, and Give one year away to others.

If I live to be one hundred years old, I hope I will have Lived on 80 years, Saved 10 years for myself, and Gave 10 years away to others. Somehow this formula for a life time seems to balance. It shows me the big picture of God's intention for my life. It gives me a measuring rod upon which I can assess how I am doing. Our lives are measured by time, in the course of which we change, grow old and, as with all living beings on earth, we die. Death is the end of time for earthly life. I believe if I follow this formula, I will be invited to enter the gates of heaven to live eternally with Jesus. Let us remember that time is not our own, but rather a gift from God and therefore, let us be a good steward of time and Live on 80%, Save 10% and Give 10% to others.

Grow Vigorously & Thrive

- The word tithe means a tenth of one's income paid to a church.
- I believe this tithe — this holy calculation — is not mine to understand or be able to calculate because it resides in the spiritual kingdom.
- This kingdom is the Lord's and everything in it belongs to Him, including time and money.
- The time tithing formula gives me a measuring rod upon which I can assess how I am doing.
- I believe if I follow this formula, I will be invited to enter the gates of heaven to live eternally with Jesus.
- Let us be a good steward of time and Live on 80%, Save 10% and Give 10% to others.

CHAPTER EIGHT

Time is a Trainer

If God predetermines the events of life — *"There is an appointed time for everything"* (Ecclesiastes 3:1) — why am I running around so busy trying to plan my days, weeks, months and years? If God has already appointed time for everything, then who am I to alter His plans for my life? Who am I to plan out every last minute of the day without first consulting Him to make sure I'm following His path for my life?

We are created by God as human beings. Instead of asking, "What am I going to do today?" I should ask myself, "How am I going to be today?" God didn't create us as human doings. He created us as human beings. I am just supposed to be, in Christ Jesus with every moment of my life. *Just be.* But what does that even mean? Isaiah 40:30-31 says, *"Though youths grow weary and tired, and vigorous young men stumble badly, yet those who wait for the Lord will gain new strength; they will mount up with wings like eagles, they will run and not get tired, they will walk and not become weary."* The message here is to wait for the Lord. When we are young, we have a tendency to go full speed ahead toward our dream, goal or vision of success. We work hard and vigorously plan every ounce of time, unknowingly or purposely robbing ourselves of sleep, health, and energy. This goes on year after year as we sprint toward our definition of success.

At first everything seems new, exciting, and adventurous. Then, certain tasks and events become repetitive, and the newness settles into the everyday routine. What used to be the pursuit of a dream becomes a labor to survive and pay the bills. Eventually we stumble and grow weary and tired. We exhaust our own vain efforts and throw in the towel, look up to heaven and wonder, isn't there more to life than this? I've experienced this in my own life. I was married at 22 and had my first child at 25. I started my business at 26 and had my second child at 27. I had a drive and a passion for my family and was chasing the American dream. My kids began to grow as well as my business. Over a 15 year period, the kids got busy in school and the business grew to over $2 million in annual revenue. The kids were each three-sport athletes and I employed 23 people, owned a large facility, an 80 foot crane, a digger derrick truck, a 100 foot boom truck and multiple service vehicles. I was working hard and vigorously planning every ounce of time, unknowingly robbing myself of sleep, good health and energy. I loved what I was doing, but the stress was taking a toll on me. Life was passing me by faster than a speeding bullet. I proclaimed that my priorities were first God, then my husband, and next my kids, but the business kept sucking much of my time away.

I was working hard to be the perfect wife, mom of the year, and boss extraordinaire. That is, until I grew weary, tired, and stumbled. I could not keep up any longer. In 2007, at age 40, I hesitantly closed my business due to stress and the start of the economic recession. I could no longer support the cost of doing business — something I paid for at the expense of God and my family. Most of the stress was caused by a lack of balance surrounding my time. I became extremely depressed, realizing the negative impact closing my business had on so many families I had employed.

I lost my identity. I no longer knew who I was, what I was good at or who I was supposed to be. But the one thing that stayed constant was my deep and abiding faith that in God, all things are possible. That is what I had left. It was everything I clung to. And that is what saved me.

After six months of unemployment, I went back to work. This time though, the work was different. I had prayed for a job that was a no-brainer — a job where I didn't have to be the one in charge, or responsible if things didn't work out. God answered my prayers and gave me a job. It was not the pursuit of the American dream, it was just a job. It wasn't something I hoped to spend the rest of my life doing or something I was passionate about. It was just a job. It had no meaning, no future, and it gave me no fulfillment.

Over the years, I never stopped to acknowledge the skills and abilities I had learned. Even though this job was easy and had virtually no challenges, it sucked the very life right out of me. I had been hired by someone who only cared about his profits, not the people who worked for him. The boss extraordinaire I worked so hard to be to my former employees — by appreciating them and recognizing their achievements — was not how I was treated by my boss at this new job. In fact, it was quite the opposite. My boss ruled with an iron fist. It was his way or no way. He didn't appreciate hard work, and he certainly didn't recognize anyone, because he believed he was the only important person in the office.

I couldn't imagine why God would allow him to treat me and my coworkers so terribly. He was unfair, condescending, verbally abusive, and caused strife at every opportunity. I thought about quitting many times, but heard God's still small voice saying, "Wait, you are learning something here." And learning I was. I was learning all the ways in which not to treat people.

In the meantime, I prayed God would deliver me from this pit. I was still getting up at 5 a.m. every morning to spend time in my prayer room. The more and more time I spent reading the Bible and growing closer to Jesus, the more calm and peaceful I became in my circumstances. Even though I was being mistreated, God was protecting me. I learned what it meant to pray for my enemies. I learned what it meant to forgive people when they hurt me. I learned what it meant to trust God while I waited. I knew this was not God's plan for my life — to be stuck in a dead end job that brought me down — but I was scared to quit, fearing I wouldn't be able to contribute toward surmounting bills.

I asked myself, "How am I going to be today?" I'm going to be in Christ Jesus with every moment of my life. I'm going to praise Him and thank Him while I wait in this circumstance. I'm going to let this time be a trainer — a precious gift God has given me while I wait. I'm going to let this time allow me to know every aspect of Jesus so I may continue to fall deeper and deeper in love with him. Waiting isn't a bad thing. It's a blessing beyond measure.

So if you find yourself in an uncomfortable situation, take a deep breath, and just simply be... with Jesus. Let Him teach you and train you. Timothy 3:16-17 says, *"All Scripture is inspired by God and profitable for teaching, for reproof, for correction, for training in righteousness; that the man of God may be adequate, equipped for every good work"*. I believed the longer I had to wait, the more adequate and equipped I would be for the next job God had in store for me. In the meantime, I continued to trust my faith and keep learning and being trained in righteousness and truth by the Word of God. Time is a trainer.

Grow Vigorously & Thrive

- There is an appointed time for everything.
- God didn't create us as human doings, He created us as human beings.
- We work hard and vigorously planning every ounce of time, unknowingly or purposely robbing ourselves of sleep, health, and energy.
- I'm going to be in Christ Jesus with every moment of my life.
- I'm going to let time allow me to know every aspect of Jesus so I may continue to fall deeper and deeper in love with him.
- Waiting isn't a bad thing. It's a blessing beyond measure.

IT'S TIME ~ FLOURISH NOW

CHAPTER **9**

CHAPTER NINE

You Are Not Alone

Have you ever felt you are alone in the world? Like you have absolutely no one to turn to or who understands you? Recently, I happened upon the scripture verse Psalm 31:15 which says, *"My times are in Thy hand."* I believe this is true with my life — my times are in God's hand. *All* my time is in His hand, unless I choose to go my own way making selfish, prideful choices. In these instances, I find life seems difficult, uneasy, and unpredictable — a scary, painful way to live. Trust me, I've done it and learned the hard way that it's not worth my time not to first ask for God's council before going into my day.

Proverbs 3:9-10 says, *"Honor the Lord from your wealth* (time), *and from the first* (upon waking) *of all your produce* (time harvest); *so your barns* (minds) *will be filled with plenty* (knowledge of the presence of Jesus), *and your vats* (hearts) *will overflow with new wine* (love)." My interpretation of time in the verse (noted in parentheses) is what I believe God wants me to do with my time. When I wake up each day the "first" time I spend from my harvest (or my whole day), needs to honor the Lord. If I honor the Lord first with my time, I can expect my mind to be filled with the love of Jesus. He will be in the forefront of my mind throughout my day, guiding me in doing what is right. I can expect my heart to overflow with new love I would not otherwise have if I didn't take the first time of my day to spend with Jesus. Instead, He rewards me with abundant peace and love, allowing me to share it with others throughout my day.

I have also come to realize that it's not enough to just allow the presence of Jesus to be with me in that first time in the morning. I must also learn to turn my focus on the presence of Jesus throughout the day. He helps me decipher right from wrong in my decisions and behaviors in each moment. The minute my mind wanders from Jesus' presence into unchartered, selfish territory — and doesn't take into consideration what Jesus wants me to do with my time — I feel myself sinking and failing in simple decisions or behavioral responses toward others. I react with pride, criticism, selfishness, complaints, victim mentality and the like. Jesus does not want this for me, but He allows it so that I may learn from it and ultimately turn my focus back to Him, guiding me in every moment. When I keep my focus on Jesus' presence, my choice is to instinctively do the right thing, whether I feel like it or not.

Earlier in the book I explained that feelings are fickle, and we cannot rely on them to rule our minds and hearts. Isaiah 26:3 says; *"The steadfast of mind Thou wilt keep in perfect peace."* What this means to me is if I fix my mind constantly on Jesus, I will keep in perfect peace. Now *that* is freedom. That is what I strive for. That is what I long for. Perfect peace in this life is what Jesus intends for me to have if only I harness myself to His constant presence within me. If only I always seek His counsel. If only I bite my tongue and refuse to speak words or make gestures that hurt others. It is then that I can expect to be in perfect peace, thanks to my good behavior.

This is the battle I fight every day: to put Jesus first in my mind and heart. It's about having the strength to willfully and purposefully guard my words and actions so as not only to maintain the freedom that comes with perfect peace, but also sustain the freedom indefinitely. I am a long way from enjoying freedom in all my moments because I am still weak in my humanity. Just this morning I found myself weeping and asking Jesus for forgiveness for how I had behaved toward others yesterday. We live in a broken world around other broken people who lash out and don't know or have the understanding of Jesus and how their very peace, joy and freedom in life is dependent on knowing Him and abiding in His presence. Therefore people around us lash out, gossip, backstab, and deceive. In my human weakness, I reacted to their behavior by lashing back instead of holding my tongue, taking a deep breath and asking Jesus for His wise counsel. Once again I was humbled — and sad — about my choice to react instead of staying in the presence of Jesus and allowing Him to fight the battle for me.

The more I practice staying in the presence of Jesus, the more peace I've begun to experience. As a result, I'm beginning to really enjoy life and understand why Jesus wants me to use my will to make the choice to love at all times. I've found that the only person I truly hurt when I choose to lash out and react negatively is me. I cannot feel what others feel, I cannot think what others think, and cannot do what others do. But I have the power to change what I think, feel, and do. My power comes from my faith and trust in Jesus. He has taught me, scolded me, corrected me, protected me, trusted me, justified me, valued me, and loved me. I have put all my trust in Him to help me continue to grow in willfully making right choices in His presence — all in the longing for perfect peace.

So where does this "presence of Jesus" come from and exist? Jesus' presence comes from spending time with Him in prayer, thanksgiving, submission, requests, and in His presence. The presence of Jesus also comes from spending time studying His words in the Bible. The more time I've spent studying scripture, the more I understand the real truth. It's not the "truth" the media and world wants me to believe, but the real, life-giving truth that Jesus died to give me and you.

Each and every word in the Bible has great meaning that I can apply to my daily life, helping me grow in my walk with Jesus. Where does the presence of Jesus exist? He exists in my heart — in my innermost being. I can feel His love swelling within me, so much so that His presence is hard to contain. The more I know Him and the love He has for me, the more I cannot help but allow it to overflow to others I interact with. It is a joy beyond explanation. His presence is knowing through faith — being sure of what I hope for and certain of what I do not see — that He is with me. He is not in the past, and He is not in the future. He is with me in this very moment, in the present.

Therefore, I must also stay in this moment in order to receive His help, guidance, and love. I must keep my mind and heart out of anything that's happened in the past and discipline myself to trust that Jesus has my future already planned out. I must stop convincing myself I'm a better planner than Him. It's in this moment that I find my peace. It's in this moment that I find joy. It's in this moment, with Jesus, that I can handle the time I've been given.. If I try to go back in the past or skip forward to the future, it's too big, too much, and too scary for me. But, if I remain in this moment — in the presence of Jesus — I can manage and control it.

Jesus counsels me on how to manage and control this moment. I've learned to seek His counsel before speaking or taking action in the moment. (Although, let's be honest, I cannot say I've mastered it yet.) Even as I sit here writing at 12:49 p.m., I'm still in my pajamas and robe and have anxiety that I should have long been up and dressed, accomplishing everything on my to-do list for the day. But, I am fighting the battle to obey Jesus, and today I felt Him prompting me to write.

So, I put aside my selfish desire to get dressed and working today. Instead I chose to listen to His still small voice in hopes that in some small way, my battle will help you to realize the importance of spending time in the presence of Jesus. Get to know Him. Spend time in His word, the Bible. Spend time talking to Him in a normal conversation in the car, lying in bed or in line at the grocery store. Be silent and feel His loving presence engulf your heart and mind.

Getting to know Jesus takes time, just like it does when you get to know a stranger. Don't expect immediate results or to know Him personally in one short sitting. Repetition is the mother of skill, and I have repeatedly spent time with Jesus throughout many years. Still, I cannot seem to get enough time with Him. I am so deeply in love with Him and the truth He longs to share with me. I pray that each and every one of you that reads this chapter makes a commitment to spend the "first" part of your day with Jesus, and take His presence with you. You will find that your days seem lighter, your peace more abundant, your freedom readily available, and your joy overflowing. Don't you think a small investment of your time is worth these amazing rewards? There is peace in the presence of Jesus that is beyond understanding. Take it. It's yours to have right now. You are not alone.

Grow Vigorously & Thrive

- If I honor the Lord first with my time, I can expect my mind to be filled with the love of Jesus.
- I must also learn to turn my focus on the presence of Jesus throughout the day.
- Perfect peace in this life is what Jesus intends for me to have if only I harness myself to His constant presence within me.
- The more I practice staying in the presence of Jesus, the more peace I've begun to experience.
- Jesus is with me in this very moment, in the present. There is peace in the presence of Jesus that is beyond understanding.
- Be silent and feel His loving presence engulf your heart and mind.

CHAPTER TEN

Now Is the Acceptable Time

Is now the acceptable time? Can I have peace *right now* in any circumstance? Why does it seem so hard to believe? How can I have peace in the midst of my problems? Why does it seem so hard to achieve?

The answer is: it's due to my weakness in the battle to control my mind. Thankfully, with the help of the Holy Spirit, peace can be mine in all moments. I just must ask Him to control my thoughts and actions. And when I do, I'll be blessed with life and peace. Let's be realistic—there will still be difficulties along the way, but its how I choose to react to each difficulty that will produce either turmoil or peace. The secret to peace is giving thanks for each trial that arises. Many times throughout my day I recite the words, "Thank you, Lord Jesus, and praise You. Thank you, Lord Jesus, and praise Your holy name." Even during hardships and trials, I confidently recite my praises, knowing He can turn every difficulty into a blessing. By thanking Him, I relinquish my fear, anger, and frustration to Him and engage my faith by believing I've already received the fruits of trusting Him in all circumstances. Even right in the midst of the difficulties, I trust Him for blessings and rewards for praising His holy name.

Ten years ago my sister was diagnosed with large B cell lymphoma. The cancer had almost completely eaten away her hip socket. In my desperation at the thought of losing her, I entered a chapel. My first inclination was to fervently pray for her healing. In that very moment I felt the overwhelming love of God rain down on me with confidence that my humble heartfelt, tear-filled prayer had been answered. My second prayer was; "Thank you, Lord Jesus and praise You. Thank you, Lord and praise Your holy name." Today my sister is completely healed of cancer and the bone in her hip socket has grown back in its' original form.

Now Is the Acceptable Time

II Corinthians 6:1-10 describes this recipe in detail." *And working together with Him we also urge you not to receive the grace of God in vain- for He says, "At the acceptable time I listened to you, and on the day of salvation I helped you"; behold, now is "the acceptable time," behold, now is "the day of salvation" — giving no cause for offense in anything, in order that the ministry be not discredited, but in everything commending ourselves as servants of God, in much endurance, in afflictions, in hardships, in distresses, in beatings, in imprisonments, in tumults, in labors, in sleeplessness, in hunger, in purity, in knowledge, in patience, in kindness, in the Holy Spirit, in genuine love, in the word of truth, in the power of God; by the weapons of righteousness for the right hand and the left, by glory and dishonor, by evil report and good report; regarded as deceivers and yet true: as unknown yet well-known, as dying yet behold, we live; as punished yet not put to death, as sorrowful yet always rejoicing, as poor yet making many rich, as having nothing yet possessing all things.*

This clearly states that I can have peace in *all* circumstances. It gives me answers as to how God teaches me to respond to suffering. I cannot have peace on my own accord, but only through the help of the Holy Spirit can I find the treasure of peace. Isaiah 33:6 states, *"And He shall be the stability of your times, a wealth of salvation, wisdom, and knowledge; the fear of the Lord is his treasure."* I am to fear the Lord so as not to do what is wrong and punishable by Him. But I'm also not to live in fear. Isaiah 41:10 states, *"Do not fear, for I am with you; Do not anxiously look about you, for I am your God. I will strengthen you, surely I will help you, surely I will uphold you with My righteous right hand."*

In my sister's circumstance, once I had prayed for her, I deliberately made the choice to not fear the outcome or be anxious for the reports, instead I relied on God every step of the way to strengthen me and help me to continue to believe that she was healed.

Now is the acceptable time to be at peace in all my circumstances for my God is with me. Isaiah 40:28-31 clearly states, *"Do you not know? Have you not heard? The Everlasting God, the Lord, the Creator of the ends of the earth does not become weary or tired. His understanding is inscrutable. He gives strength to the weary, and to him who lacks might He increases power. Though youths grow weary and tired, and vigorous young men stumble badly, Yet those who wait for the Lord Will gain new strength; They will mount up with wings like eagles, They will run and not get tired, They will walk and not become weary."*

This tells me not to fear or be anxious in my circumstances, but rather believe my Almighty God who does not become weary or tired, will change my circumstances. My role is to wait for the Lord who will renew my strength. I can have peace right now in all circumstances by simply waiting. This is what God asks me to do — to wait and trust Him. In my waiting, I'll smile and say, "Thank you, Lord Jesus, and praise You. Thank you, Lord Jesus, and praise Your holy name." Now is the acceptable time to be at peace.

Grow Vigorously & Thrive

- With the help of the Holy Spirit, peace can be mine in all moments.
- Even during hardships and trials, I confidently recite my praises, knowing He can turn every difficulty into a blessing.
- I cannot have peace on my own accord, but only through the help of the Holy Spirit can I find the treasure of peace.
- I can have peace right now in all circumstances by simply waiting.
- Now is the acceptable time to be at peace.

CHAPTER ELEVEN

Time Is The Period Between Two Eternities

What is time anyway? The definition states it's the period between two eternities — the state or fact of being without beginning or end. It's a long period that seems endless. And yet, I seem to own my time. Time is always with me... but I am taught time is not my own. Time has been given to me as a precious gift from God. If time is a gift, then I ought to look forward to it. If time is a gift, I ought to feel blessed by receiving it from someone who loves me. If time is a gift, I should cherish it and make the most of it. It has a purpose. Time is given to me for my pleasure. Time is given to me for my enjoyment. Time is given to me to discover the beauty that lies within it. Time has a purpose.

I imagine all of the people in world who don't comprehend this truth and would just as soon waste it away rather than to cultivate it. It's a shame to not know how life-giving this gift of time is when used properly. I pray that you will cultivate this precious gift so that it will grow and flourish and you will be blessed.

II Peter 3:8-10 says, *"But do not let this one fact escape your notice, beloved, that with the Lord one day is as a thousand years, and a thousand years as one day. The Lord is not slow about His promise, as some count slowness, but is patient toward you, not wishing for any to perish but for all to come to repentance. But the day of the Lord will come like a thief, in which the heavens will pass away with a roar and the elements will be destroyed with intense heat, and the earth and its works will be burned up."*

Time is given to me to discover the Lord's promises. The Lord has promised me salvation. The Lord has promised to graciously accept in Christ all repenting sinners. This means a Christian has the right to be in heaven someday, for he is in Christ. God promises He will work out all things for our good. Jesus has promised us eternal life and abundant life. This covers not only our final destiny in heaven, but also our present Christian service here on earth. He is, in fact, right now praying for us at His Father's right hand. The promise of the Holy Spirit is said to dwell in the believer.

He places all believing sinners into the body of Christ, thus assuring us of His union with God Himself. Wow, now *that* is a promise I can place hope in. But I must do my part. Abundant life is mine to have at this very moment, but I must repent my sins, turn away from wrongdoing and walk on the path of righteousness as Jesus has taught me. By doing this, God has guaranteed He will work out all things for our good. Time for God is of no value. One day is as a thousand years, and a thousand years is as one day. This tells me God is patient — that He is willing to wait a thousand years for me to repent and come back to him. And yet, it also tells me that even though my sins have been so great and practiced over an extended amount of time, God will count a thousand years as one day for me. This is how much my God loves me. He forgives even the most hardened hearts. What a gift this is. Instead of living in darkness, sin, and death, in one split second, I can repent my sins and live in the light, purity, and life that God promised me. Oh what joy! What saving grace! Oh to be loved by a generous and forgiving God!

II Peter 3:13 says, *"But according to His promise we are looking for new heavens and a new earth, in which righteousness dwells. Therefore, beloved, since you look for these things, be diligent to be found by Him in peace, spotless and blameless, and regard the patience of our Lord to be salvation."* So what should I be doing with this precious gift of time that God has bestowed upon me? Time seems like an eternity and yet as if it is one day, depending on circumstances beyond my control. God predetermines the events of life in Ecclesiastes 3:1-15 which states, *"There is an appointed time for everything. And there is a time for every event under heaven —*

> *A time to give birth, and a time to die;*
> *A time to plant, and a time to uproot what is planted.*
> *A time to kill, and a time to heal;*
> *A time to tear down and a time to build up.*
> *A time to weep, and a time to laugh;*
> *A time to mourn, and a time to dance.*
> *A time to throw stones, and a time to gather stones,*
> *A time to embrace, and a time to shun embracing.*
> *A time to search, and a time to give up as lost;*
> *A time to keep, and a time to throw away,*
> *A time to tear apart, and a time to sew together,*
> *A time to be silent, and a time to speak.*
> *A time to love, and a time to hate;*
> *A time for war and a time for peace."*

This tells me I should carefully balance how I spend my time, and yet time is not mine to control. I cannot control it, but I can react appropriately to every given moment. Tipping the scale this way or that or maintaining a righteous, loving-kindness, I can create the perfect balance in order to live in peace and receive the promises given to me by God. Thank you, Lord Jesus, for this precious gift of time for me to enjoy with You. Thank you for the knowledge that only in You, your joy may be complete in me. Thank you Lord Jesus for saving me from myself and thank you for every event under heaven. Thank you Lord, for teaching me that I can have abundant peace and joy in this period between two eternities.

Grow Vigorously & Thrive

- If time is a gift, I should cherish it and make the most of it.
- Time is given to me to discover the beauty that lies within it.
- Time is given to me to discover the Lord's promises.
- Thank you Lord Jesus, for this precious gift of time for me to enjoy with You.
- Thank you for the knowledge that only in You, your joy may be complete in me.
- Thank you, Lord, for teaching me that I can have abundant peace and joy in this period between two eternities.

CHAPTER TWELVE

Planning is a Waste of Time

How many times do I have to learn time is not my own? How many times does God have to teach me the same lesson before I stop, listen and obey Him in order to receive the life He already has planned for me? My life is not my own. It's God's. Not until I acknowledge the fact that I'm a passenger meant to enjoy the ride — not the driver trying to control my every turn — will I be able to be at peace in every moment. God makes this clear in Ephesians 5:15, saying, *"Therefore be careful how you walk, not as unwise men, but as wise, making the most of your time, because the days are evil. So then do not be foolish, but understand what the will of the Lord is."*

I think in order to understand what the will of the Lord is, we need to be in close communion with Him and listening carefully to the promptings of our hearts. Not foolishly thinking that we know everything by head knowledge alone. But rather, through emotional intelligence we find the will of God. Emotional intelligence is the capacity to be aware of, control, and express one's emotions, and to handle interpersonal relationships judiciously and empathetically. This is where the connection to the heart is. If we are not in tune with our emotions and that of other people, it is difficult to be in tune with the will of God.

Often I misunderstand "making the most of your time" as needing to plan the day. But just prior to this is the warning "be careful how you walk, not as unwise men, but as wise". An unwise man is someone who does not have or does not show good judgement, whereas a wise man is someone who is informed by God. God advises "do not be foolish," because the days are evil. It's imperative I understand the will of God in my life, so I don't fall into sin and temptation and waste this precious gift of time God has given me to discover.

But what exactly is God's will for me? And how do I understand what that is? Ephesians 5:18 says, *"And do not get drunk with wine, for that is dissipation, but be filled with the spirit."* The first part of the verse warns us what not to do. It tells us not to indulge in pleasure to the point of harming our self. This is followed by what we should do. We should be filled with the Spirit which is to be controlled by the Spirit and is therefore crucial to successfully doing the will of God. Unlike the dwelling of the Spirit, filling is a repeated experience. This is underscored by the use of the present tense ("be filled") as well as by Biblical examples of Christians who were filled more than once. Just as important, we must observe that filling is a command, not an option. To be filled is to deliberately take in or consume until full. This is an action that I must choose to do. The action is to spend time in prayer, reading the Bible, and focusing on what God's will is for how I should spend my time.

When I stated that planning is a waste of time, I meant that if I plan out my day, I don't allow God to take control. I don't allow myself to be filled with the Spirit or to submit my time to Him first. Instead I try to do it alone without consulting Him. I try to take control of my day, my way.

The next most important question is: how can I be filled with the Spirit? Through the confession of my sin and the dedicating of myself to God, I am filled with the Spirit and able to show plainly Christ-like character. The certainty of being filled with the Spirit may be confirmed by my faith and life. I must believe God's Word that meeting the conditions will result in the filling. The Spirit-filled person will exhibit the Christ-like character described in Galatians 5:22, 23: *"But the fruit of the Spirit is love, joy, peace, patience, kindness, goodness, faithfulness, gentleness, self-control"*. That list includes all the vibrant, attractive qualities desired by all Christians. How delightful it is that any Christian may possess them and be transformed by the filling of the Spirit.

How do I know I'm proceeding carefully into my day, walking wisely, making the most of my time, and understanding the will of the Lord? The simple answer is to be filled with the Spirit. This is the longing of my heart. I search for this as I selfishly plan my day away. It's no wonder I have regrets after planning a day my way. I inadvertently take away the precious time God has gifted me and put in its place a fruitless waste of time, searching for what already exists. If I but trust, wait patiently, and listen for God's still small voice moment by moment, I might find my peace.

Today I fully receive love, joy, peace, patience, kindness, goodness, faithfulness, gentleness and self-control. Today I wait in joyful hope for the coming of Jesus Christ in my day. Today I dedicate myself to God's perfect will. No longer will I waste away my days with planning and anxiety. I will simply wait on the Lord in each moment. I will enjoy my life. I will be at peace with whatever situation arises. Yes, Lord, I will listen for Your plan for my life. I can handle this moment with You. Outside of this moment, You do not exist, therefore I will find peace in this moment with You. I will not wander alone into the dessert of my own planning. I will trust in Your perfect will. I will be calm. I know without Your guidance, planning is a waste of time.

Grow Vigorously & Thrive

- The problem with planning is I think I know better than what God has in store for me.
- In order to understand what the will of the Lord is, we need to be in close communion with Him.
- Do not be foolish, but understand what the will of the Lord is.
- It's imperative I understand the will of God in my life, so I don't fall into sin and temptation.
- To be filled with the Spirit is to deliberately take in or consume until full.
- Through the confession of my sin and the dedicating of myself to God, I am filled with the Spirit.
- The fruit of the Spirit is love, joy, peace, patience, kindness, goodness, faithfulness, gentleness, self-control.
- I will simply wait on the Lord in each moment.

Planning is a Waste of Time

IT'S TIME ~ FLOURISH NOW

CHAPTER THIRTEEN

Do Not Worry About Tomorrow's Time Today

Have you ever had anxiety about what lies ahead? Or been worried that you will not be equipped to handle what might happen tomorrow? Matthew 6:34 says, *"Therefore do not be anxious for tomorrow: for tomorrow will care for itself. Each day has enough trouble of its own."* I love this verse, because it holds profound truth. The problem, however, lies in *how* to do it. I long for the peace it promises. It reads as a command saying, "do not be anxious for tomorrow," and yet it doesn't come that simple for me. When anxious thoughts and worries have their grasp on me, they manifest themselves in a physical way by tightening the muscles around my shoulders and neck and pulling tight on the base of my skull, creating a subtle, cloudy thinking process. My heart begins to beat in a dizzying, racing pattern, and my eyes scurry back and forth wildly as if watching an intense tennis match. And yet, in the midst of this physical calamity, I am commanded, "do not be anxious for tomorrow." Period.

The first thing I must do is trust. I must trust God will take care of my tomorrow. After all, He states in Matthew 6:26-27, *"Look at the birds of the air, that they do not sow, neither do they reap, nor gather into barns, and yet, your heavenly Father feeds them. Are you not worth much more than they? And which of you by being anxious can add a single cubit to his life's span?"* By trusting God will take care of tomorrow, I release myself from the heavy burden of thoughts lingering into time that has not yet occurred. Only then can I float back into the present, singular moment that not only promises the peace I long for, but actually provides it. When I deliberately choose to refuse thoughts of tomorrow, I'm catapulted back from the unknown future and into the present moment. There I can be fully immersed with the ability to touch, taste, see, hear, and smell with my imagination intact and the rhythm of my heart in sync with the beauty of the world around me. This doesn't mean the present moment won't have troubles and challenges. It means the present moment is manageable for my mind if I choose to trust God for His providence as stated in Matthew 6:33 *"seek first His kingdom and His righteousness; and all these things shall be added to you."*

I can have peace in the present moment, regardless of my circumstances. I have learned when I begin to feel anxious; I've allowed my imagination to drift into the future where I feel naked, vulnerable, alone, insecure, and unable to foresee answers in this dangerous, unchartered territory.

I'm now able to assess the onset of anxious thoughts, hold them captive, and shift back to the present moment by simply asking myself, "Where are you right now?" And then realize where I am and what I'm doing in the moment.

By asking myself this question, I'm choosing to leave the unchartered territory and return home to God who is in the present moment. This truth is found in Psalm 46:1, *"God is our refuge and strength, a very present help in trouble."* The word "present" means existing or happening *now,* not in the future. God is our help *now.* He's our refuge and protection from the danger of *now*. He is our strength right *now*. We do not need to rely on our own strength in the present moment, because it's in this moment that God exists. God says in Isaiah 41:10, *"Do not fear, for I am with you; Do not anxiously look about you, for I am your God. I will strengthen you, surely I will help you. Surely I will uphold you with My righteous right hand."*

Praise God who is with me in this very moment. Praise God who I can rely on when I am weak, for He is my strength in this moment. Praise God who gives me peace regardless of my circumstances. Praise God who tells me it's time — in this present moment — to flourish now. Do not wait for tomorrow to enjoy your life while you waste today in worry and anxiety. Take captive your thoughts and choose to enjoy every single moment God has gifted you by starting right now. Now is the time to flourish — to grow vigorously and thrive in this present moment with God who is your refuge and strength. Do not worry about tomorrow's time today. The time to enjoy your life is now.

Grow Vigorously & Thrive

- Do not be anxious for tomorrow: for tomorrow will care for itself.
- By trusting God will take care of tomorrow, I release myself from the heavy burden of thoughts lingering into time that has not yet occurred.
- The present, singular moment not only promises the peace I long for, but actually provides it.
- In the present, I can be fully immersed with the ability to touch, taste, see, hear, and smell with my imagination intact and the rhythm of my heart in sync with the beauty of the world around me.
- God is our help *now*.
- We do not need to rely on our own strength in the present moment because it's in this moment God exists.
- Praise God who tells me it's time — in this present moment — to flourish now.

- Do not wait for tomorrow to enjoy your life while you waste today in worry and anxiety.
- Take captive your thoughts and choose to enjoy every single moment God has gifted you.

CHAPTER FOURTEEN

A Time For Contentment

What does it mean to be content anyway? According to the dictionary definition it says "happy with one's lot, fate, portion or fortune." To be content is to live in a state of peaceful happiness. This is something I desperately crave but struggle to accept. I can't help but wonder if I should be doing more (or something different) than what I'm doing in the present moment. Is God expecting more from me? Am I contributing the most I can to those around me? How am I making a difference by sharing Christ with enough people so they are guaranteed salvation? Could I be doing more? These are questions that I continually ask myself as the days, months and years pass by. When I get to heaven, will God say, "Well done, good and faithful servant"?

These questions continue to shake my contentment in the present moments of each day. I find myself discontent and sometimes even dissatisfied with how I chose to spend my time as my doubts surface, asking if there was something more meaningful I could have done.

In my great desire to please God with my time, I realize my discontentment stems from the notion that I must *do* something in order to please God. This notion assumes God has great expectations of what I should be doing, accomplishing, or achieving. But this is another lie from Satan. It's Satan's way of stealing peace from the present moment, trying to convince me I'm not busy enough and God won't be pleased if I don't race after a man-made success ideal. Satan wants to keep me so busy running after success that I can't hear God's still small voice whispering, "Rest in My peace."

God tells me exactly what He wants me to do in Philippians 4:6-9 saying, *"Be anxious for nothing, but in everything by prayer and supplication with thanksgiving let your requests be made known to God. And the peace of God, which surpasses all comprehension, shall guard your hearts and your minds in Christ Jesus. Finally, brethren, whatever is true, whatever is honorable, whatever is right, whatever is pure, whatever is lovely, whatever is of good repute, if there is anything worthy of praise, let your mind dwell on these things. The things you have learned and received and heard and seen in Me, practice these things; and the God of peace shall be with you."*

This scripture says it all. This is the truth my aching heart needed to hear. I don't need to strive to please God by accomplishing things. Rather, I must simply let my mind dwell on things that please God. It has more to do with taking control of my mind and remaining in peace in order to be content. The mind is a wild, complex, beast that must be harnessed and brought into control by grabbing hold of thoughts and either casting them out of your mind if they are not righteous or dwelling on them if they are. After practicing this over and over, I'm able to feel God's loving peace in the present moment. I can have peace in all circumstances if I tame the wild beast of my mind into a gentle, peaceful creature that bathes in the sun of God's almighty love for me.

Philippians 4:12-13 reads, *"I know how to get along with humble means, and I also know how to live in prosperity; in any and every circumstance I have learned the secret of being filled and going hungry, both of having abundance and suffering need. I can do all things through Him who strengthens me."* With this scripture, I've chosen to be content in all circumstances by taking every negative thought captive and deliberately casting it out of my mind, returning to dwell on blessings I'm thankful for.

My life has been changed since I began using this tool. Every negative thought can be replaced with something I am grateful for whether it is a person or my circumstance. By merely being thankful I choose to completely change my feeling toward someone or the situation. I highly recommend putting this into practice. But I must warn you, that it takes time and patience. However, if you stick with it and make a deliberate attempt not to engage in hurtful gossip but instead have a kind word to say, or when you fear a pending circumstance may have a terrible outcome but instead thank God for his presence in that moment, you will find peace and contentment. This is truly a life changing endeavor.

I've learned to practice the art of mind control in order to gain contentment and happiness in my life. God wants me to experience peace and joy right now — in this very moment and in every moment. This is God's will for me. This is what pleases God. This is what I can do in order to please God: I can take control of my mind in all circumstances and trust, through faith that God is here with me now. I can quit searching and running after my ideal of success because I've already arrived right here, right now. This is the time for contentment.

Grow Vigorously & Thrive

- Whatever is true, whatever is honorable, whatever is right, whatever is pure, whatever is lovely, whatever is of good repute, if there is anything worthy of praise, let your mind dwell on these things.
- I don't need to strive to please God by accomplishing things.
- I must simply let my mind dwell on things that please God.
- It has more to do with taking control of my mind and remaining in peace in order to be content.
- Practice the art of mind control in order to gain contentment and happiness in your life.

CHAPTER FIFTEEN

God Is Master Of Time

The mind is my memory, opinion, and the seat of consciousness in which thinking and feeling take place. It's my intellect, psyche, reason and sanity. And, although I feel I have a close, personal relationship with my mind, often times I feel like I'm out of my mind all together. As I look back on life and think about the times I felt furthest from God, it was when I allowed my mind to convince me life wasn't going to be okay. I was lured by Satan to believe my future was doomed. The wild beast of my mind had taken control and proved to me (or so I thought) there was no way out. Surely my future was hopeless, and there was nothing I could do about it. Depression is debilitating.

It's as though I had been picked up by a rabid, snarling dog that violently shook its head in attempt to weaken, debilitate, and incapacitate my power to go on. Once the wild beast of my mind had shaken me to the core of hopelessness, it dropped me there and I no longer had any power left to think. Satan had conquered, as I lay curled up in a ball, unable to move. My mind had convinced me my future was lost. I didn't have the strength, will power or hope to go on. Moving was not an option as my weakness gave way to despair, and I feared any movement would arouse the wild beast. I reasoned that if I just played dead and tried to stay asleep, I wouldn't have to deal with the ugly truth of my circumstances.

The wild beast kept on and on with questions like, "How did I get here? Why did this happen to me? How do I go on?" These questions conjured up answers I'd rehearse over and over, replaying a state of despair for what seemed like forever. My family gathered around me to pray for healing and hope. I could not believe I'd created this type of concern. I was ashamed, embarrassed, and defeated — just another vice Satan was using to keep me from going on. I knew somehow, someway, I needed to escape from the dark horror. Satan had stolen my joy.

Then, after a lengthy period in this solitary confinement, the right question emerged. How can I get control of this situation? The incredible thing about the mind is that it'll always search for answers to the questions you ask it. It was the right question, because it allowed me to search through the library of my mind for an answer that caused me to take one step forward. The answer I found was in Philippians 4:13, *"I can do all things through Christ who strengthens me."* This answer was the little morsel of hope that I needed. It was just enough light for me to dare to hope I could do something about my situation. As I began to repeat this over and over in my mind, I began to take back control of the wild beast. Each time I would say, "I can do all things through Christ who strengthens me," I became convinced it was true. I began to realize my future wasn't doomed. I was reminded God is in control of my future, and all I needed to think about was the present moment. Each time my mind would try to scare me into thinking about the future, I would cast the thoughts out.

You see, to cast a thought out of the mind is a great weapon for daily life. Defined as "to throw with force or to hurl", it basically equates to "thinking on purpose." For example, if a negative thought enters my mind — "You are a lowly, good for nothing, human being that deserves to suffer." — I recognize this thought would only come from Satan and I have the ability to stop and cast it out of my mind. I recoil, saying, "Satan, you are a liar and a thief. You come only to kill, steal, and destroy. I won't allow you to steal my joy in this moment." By purposely casting the negative thought out of my mind, I've opened it up to receive the positive truth found in Philippians 4:13, "I can do all things through Christ who strengthens me."

This allowed me to slowly but surely gain the strength I needed to face each day. It reassured me that I wasn't alone, and no matter what happened, I was equipped to handle the situation.

God gave us the power to control our thoughts. Unfortunately we are not taught this life-saving technique in school. Instead, we think our feelings control our mind, and we allow any type of feeling — whether good or bad — to take hold of our precious moments. Do you ever wonder why some people seem to always have a positive attitude, regardless of the situation? The reason is because they've learned to take control of every thought by casting away negative ones and replacing them with a positive truth filled with hope. This is how you can not only take control of the wild beast of the mind, but eventually tame it. Soon that rabid, snarling dog that weakens my power becomes my most cherished pet, greeting me with unconditional love and a spirit of joy to explore and discover the beauty that awaits me in the future.

It is so freeing to understand and put into practice this tool. The Bible has so many powerful verses that can replace bad thoughts and nourish you with life giving convictions. It has been given to us as an incredible tool to use in our daily life. I pray that you will be able to tame the wild beast and take back time Satan has stolen from you with negative thoughts and arm yourself with God's Word.

After all, "I can do all things through Christ who strengthens me." Armed with this truth, God has equipped me to master the practice of replacing fear with hope. It's time to quit believing the lies of Satan and trust that God is master of my time. It's time I learn this lesson to create a joy-filled future. It's time I share this knowledge with those I love so they too, can find the joy waiting for them. It's time to know the truth for how to use my time to make right choices in this busy world. It's time I exercise my will power by making right choices to obey God's commandments so I might experience the grandeur of love He has to share with me. It's time to commit my time to God and to be good steward of this precious gift He has given me. It's time to be trained in righteousness and truth by the Word of God. It's time to take His presence with me so my days seem lighter, my peace more abundant, my freedom readily available, and my joy overflowing. It's time to wait on the Lord in each moment. It is time right now to flourish. The time to enjoy my life is *right now*. It is time to take control of my mind in all circumstances and trust, through faith, that God is here with me now, in this moment. It's time to quit searching and running after my ideal of success because I have already arrived. I pray that you will make time to flourish — to grow vigorously and thrive. Remember, God is the master of your time.

May God bless you with abundant joy as you put your time and trust in Him.

Grow Vigorously & Thrive

- The right question emerged. How can I get control of this situation?
- The incredible thing about the mind is that it'll always search for answers to the questions you ask it.
- Each time I say, "I can do all things through Christ who strengthens me," I am convinced it is true.
- By purposely casting negative thoughts out of my mind, I open it up to receive positive truths.
- The Bible has so many powerful verses that can replace bad thoughts and nourish you with life giving convictions.
- It is time to take control of my mind in all circumstances and trust, through faith, that God is here with me now, in this moment.

IT'S TIME ~ FLOURISH NOW

CHAPTER SIXTEEN

The Test Of Time

Knowing that living, breathing, thinking and being present in every moment is the key to meaning, purpose and fulfillment in life, what must I do to ensure I keep laser focused in the present moment? The answer is to be in constant communion with God, sharing and exchanging intimate thoughts and feelings. His presence resides in the present, not in the past or in the future. It is in the present that I can talk with Him. God never leaves me. It is me who wanders away from Him when I don't stay focused in the present moment.

When I stay focused in the moment, exchanging my every thought and feeling with God, I find glorious meaning, abundant purpose and complete fulfillment. But, as simple as this may sound, it is not that easy. There are too many worldly distractions that turn my attention away from the beautiful moments that God has in store for me. My thoughts are easily lured away from the simple pleasures of the now.

In order to guard against wandering out of the present moment and make certain I exercise my will power to make good decisions, I must pass the test of time. The test of time is a real predictor of what I will do to make sure I spend time in a way that sets each day up for abundant success. The test begins each morning and is graded at the end of each day. Before I give the test, I would like to share a personal writing from my morning journal that revealed the test of time. This is a conversation with God in the present moment that ended the insanity. Out of it, the right question emerged, and the right answer surfaced. Here is the journal entry:

> *Dear Sweet Jesus,*
> *Thank you for this day off from work to spend with You. As I venture into the day, I have anxiety about how to spend my time for Your glory. My co-dependence begins to think of*

who I should try to please today. And yet, I want to spend the day doing what I want to do but begin to feel guilty that I'm being selfish. I know You want me to be at peace and enjoy my life. There are so many things I want to do that my head spins with excitement and yet, I don't know what to put on the top of the priority list that would be most fulfilling and fear if I choose something I will rush through it because there is more waiting for me to experience. This always fights with the things on the to-do list that are responsible and seemingly necessary to do in order to keep up and maintain a certain sense of organization in the home. The time will go by so fast and pretty soon it will be night fall and I will recount the events of the day and wonder if I spent the time the way You would have wanted me too or not. Dear God, how in the world can I please You alone and not myself or others? This is the desire of my heart. Learning to please You in every moment of the day. What does that mean and how do I decide what pleases You with my time? My time is not my own Lord – it is Yours. Please show me Your path today. Help me to know Your will for me. Show me what to do, so at the end of this day I will have done Your will and feel fulfilled, satisfied, content and at peace.

I knew God had been listening and wanted me to have a tool that would help me stay in the present because immediately following this journal writing, this question emerged: **What should I do today so at the end of this day I have spent my time doing God's Will and will truly feel fulfilled, satisfied, content, peaceful, purposeful, loved, courageous, free, pleased grateful, confident, accepted, delighted, happy, trusted, joyful, hopeful, inspired, kind and calm?**

I knew if I could answer this question, I would know, without a doubt, what I should do in order to have meaning, purpose and fulfillment in my life in each moment every day. So I broke the question down into a series of 20 questions that has become **The Test of Time.**

1. What will I do to be fulfilled?
2. What will I do to be satisfied?
3. What will I do to be content?
4. What will I do to be peaceful?
5. What will I do to be purposeful?
6. What will I do to be loved?
7. What will I do to be courageous?
8. What will I do to be free?

9. What will I do to be pleased?

10. What will I do to be grateful?

11. What will I do to be confident?

12. What will I do to be accepted?

13. What will I do to be delighted?

14. What will I do to be happy?

15. What will I do to be trusted?

16. What will I do to be joyful?

17. What will I do to be hopeful?

18. What will I do to be inspired?

19. What will I do to be kind?

20. What will I do to be calm?

By taking this Test of Time every morning, I set the day up to spend time on things that will be meaningful, give my life purpose and allow me to be fulfilled. It transforms me from a human doing into a human being and promotes my wellbeing. It gives me a mission and a goal to work towards. The answers to the test guide me in any stage or age of life. If this were the ultimate high school test that is given in order to graduate, it would provide the answers kids are in search of. They only have a small window of time to answer them before they begin a questionable field of study. The answers are also the medicine for anxiety and depression. By taking this test, I predetermine the priorities of the day, and abandoned the meaningless to-do list that never ends.

Each answer will differ from person to person, so this is a very personal test. It may be hard to answer the questions at first, but remember to ask God what His will is for you and have a conversation with Him. He will direct your thoughts to the library of your mind that is very intuitive and will be able to answer the question simply by asking it. As I began to answers these questions each day, it occurred to me that the answers outlined a plan for my life. By answering the questions, I knew I had a plan for the right things to do. I no longer had to have anxiety by not having enough time. The answers to the test helped me to abandoned things I was doing that we're a complete waste of time and energy, freeing me up to enjoy the moments. I no longer had to be depressed by having too much time on my hands. The answers helped me to embrace the plan and take action because I wanted what the plan promised to deliver. If I didn't act, I would fall back into the darkness of boredom and loneliness.

I know that answering these questions will be perplexing at first, so I want to give you my answers, so you can see an example of how the Test of Time works. Remember, your answers will differ and need to come from a place of deep contemplation. I suggest that you block out an hour, a day, a weekend or maybe even a whole week of time for yourself with nobody else around and away from distractions, to really dig deep inside in the presence of God and discover the beautiful life God has in store for you. He is waiting patiently to help you live the life you were created for.

Here are my answers for the Test of Time with explanations below each.

1. What will I do to be fulfilled? <u>Wake at 4am to spend time with God.</u>

    When I start the day out in my prayer room with God, He helps me to discern the true priorities ahead by writing down tasks and to-do's in my journal and getting them out of my head. This saves time by helping me understand what is not important and crossing those things off. This frees me up to concentrate on what I am called to do and gives me a clear focus resulting in a day of fulfillment.

2. What will I do to be satisfied? <u>Eat healthy for energy. No sweets.</u>

I find that making choices to eat healthy as opposed to unhealthy gives me a sense of satisfaction. If I make healthy choices throughout the day, I am in control and making strides toward my goals. If I make unhealthy choices by eating lots of sweets and impulsively putting things in my mouth without thought, I wind up feeling physically terrible and unsatisfied. Therefore, in order for me to be satisfied, I must make healthy choices for increased energy.

3. What will I do to be content? <u>Live in the present, not in past or future.</u>

    I know my contentment is derived from being in the presence of God at all times. He is my strength. I cannot find Him in the past or reach Him in the future. He is right here with me now in this moment. It's time to flourish now - not yesterday or tomorrow. I can be in a state of peaceful happiness and contentment in the present moment.

4. What will I do to be peaceful? <u>Get enough rest. Go to bed at 8:30pm.</u>

    As I said earlier in the book, it is imperative to get the proper amount of rest in order to be at peace. Rest restores all of the organs in the body as well as the mind. I make it a priority to get at least eight hours of sleep because I know that is what I need to be at my best and remain peaceful throughout the day.

5. What will I do to be purposeful? <u>To strive to uphold my mission.</u>

    Quite a while ago I spent time writing a personal mission statement that guides my actions and decisions: "To believe in and create freedom to flourish through the mastery of my thoughts, words and actions for the glory of God." This is my true north - the direction that I point every day. If I can master my thoughts and keep the lies of Satan from putting fear, torment and anguish in my mind by casting those thoughts out of my mind, and replace them with positive affirmations, I win the day. If I master my words, I will have attained the greatest weapon on the face of the earth. The Bible is the perfect example of how words can move generations. Words can be both spoken and unspoken. As the saying goes, "Sometimes unspoken words speak the loudest." And if I master my actions by designing my time how I want to use it and then committing and being disciplined in how I behave, I will have gained time to enjoy. My life will have meaning once again. I will be living a full and active lifestyle and be fulfilled. But, most importantly, my life will have purpose. Life is too short to be miserable. My prayer is that each one of you will design each day to your heart's desire so you can grow vigorously and thrive.

6. What will I do to be loved? <u>Read the Bible and devotionals.</u>

    The Bible is packed full of love truths. My very favorite quote is John 3:16 "For God so loved the world, that He gave His only begotten Son, that whoever believes in Him should not perish, but have eternal life." Let me break this down for your understanding:

    "God" – the greatest person

    "so loved" – the greatest devotion

    "the world" – the greatest number

    "He gave" – the greatest act

    "His only begotten Son" – the greatest gift

    "that whoever believes" – the greatest condition

    "should not perish" – the greatest mercy

    "have eternal life" – the greatest result

    I just feel so loved reflecting on this verse. I also like to read other devotionals during my morning prayer time that remind me I am loved beyond measure.

7. What will I do to be courageous? <u>Write truths in my prayer journal.</u>

   I never understood the power of the written word until I began writing in a journal. By getting all of my thoughts down on paper first thing in the morning, in the form of a letter to God, I am conversing with Him about all of my joys and struggles. It is like venting to a dear trusted friend, but even better. Knowing that He understands and gives me courage to face any circumstance head on.

8. What will I do to be free? <u>Apply the answers to the test of time.</u>

   To be free is not under the control or in the power of another. Many times the mind can fool us into thinking we are imprisoned in a circumstance beyond our control. The same mind can convince us that no matter what our circumstance is, that even in the midst of it, we are free to praise and worship God. If I apply the answers to the Test of Time, it produces endurance in my life and I can have its perfect results, lacking nothing.

9. What will I do to be pleased? <u>Drink 56 ounces of water daily.</u>

   Drinking water is a basic necessity of life, and yet it easy to choose something other to drink with all of the choices in today's world. By choosing to drink ½ my body weight in water, I am making a choice to be healthy and giving my body a basic foundational need. This pleases me.

10. What will I do to be grateful? <u>Continuously thank God during the day</u>

    "Thank you dear God and praise You. Thank you dear God and praise Your Holy Name." This is a prayer I repeat any time I find myself beginning to think negatively about a situation. It is truly amazing how staying in constant praise, makes me grateful at all times.

11. What will I do to be confident? <u>Don't have second helpings at meals.</u>

    This answer may seem a little strange, but let me explain. If I don't have an impulsive second helping at meal time, I am in control of my weight and health outcome. An old basketball coach once told me, "If you look good, you feel good, if you feel good, you play good and if you play good, you win!" It all starts with looking good, and looking good means making good eating choices. When I look and feel good physically, I am confident. When I veer from this plan and have second helpings, I begin to gain weight, feel sluggish and lazy and my confidence plummets.

12. What will I do to be accepted? <u>Accepting who I am in Christ.</u>

    It was hard for me to accept who I was as a person because I felt like I rarely lived up to the expectations of others. But when I began to understand who I am in Christ Jesus, I was able to accept myself. After all, I am a child of God. He made me. I am His creation. Who am I to not love His artwork? I accept myself because He made me in His image.

13. What will I do to be delighted? <u>Perform a deliberate act of love.</u>

    Nothing is more delightful to me then performing a deliberate act of love to others. This can be a simple smile, or a handwritten letter or even taking out the trash. It makes my heart feel good when I give from my heart to others.

14. What will I do to be happy? <u>Be true to myself not a people pleaser.</u>

   At one point in my life I found myself miserable, sad and depressed. The main cause was being a people pleaser. I was trying to make everyone in my life happy except for me. You can only last so long before you realize you can't make everyone happy. But if you try hard enough, you will literally drive yourself into depression. I learned I need to be true to myself and not please everyone else. It was an addiction that I had to break free from. But now that I have, I'm not turning back because I am happy!

15. What will I do to be trusted? <u>Don't fear what others think of me.</u>

   If I have no fear of what others think of me, then I will act and behave in a manner that is genuine and authentic, thus resulting in other people trusting me and being trust worthy. On the contrary, if I worry about what others think, I will act and behave in a way that is fake or not really who I am and others will see right through me and not trust me. My husband once asked me, "Why do you care about what other people think? You can't control whether they think good of you or bad of you so why waste your time worrying about it?" Brilliant. Simple. Profound. Brilliant.

16. What will I do to be joyful? <u>Act on God's calling on my life.</u>

    When I act on God's calling for my life, I am filled with joy. I am doing what He created me to do. It is such a natural part of my being that it is easy, light and fulfilling. It is not hard, it isn't work, it is just becoming more of who I was created to be. The only thing I should be doing is making an absolute commitment to feel joy - pure, true joy. Martha Beck

17. What will I do to be hopeful? <u>Be certain of what I do not see. Faith.</u>

    Faith is being sure of what you hope for and certain of what you do not see. This is very reassuring and filled with so much hope. For example, maybe I don't know how I am going to pay a bill because I don't have the money. If I be sure that the bill will be taken care of, even though I can't see how, I am releasing the problem to God who is all seeing and knowing and I engage my faith, believing it has already been taken care of. The more I exercise my faith, the more hopeful I am and the more I am certain that the positive result will be delivered. Being sure of what I hope for and certain of what I do not see. That's faith. I trust God and be certain, without doubt that He will provide. I have prayed many bold specific prayers asking God for His provision that He answered in perfect ways when I've taken this leap of faith.

18. What will I do to be inspired? <u>Learn something new every day.</u>

    Learning is the secret to an inspired life. Everyone has the ability to learn. Learn a new skill. Study a new topic. Master a new language.

    When we engage our minds to learn something new we are inspired by the newness and knowledge we gain. I have vowed to be a lifelong learner so I can stay inspired up to my final day.

19. What will I do to be kind? <u>Smile on purpose even if I don't feel like it.</u>

    Smiling is a mutually beneficial action. It is a welcome sight for the person receiving it and it causes a positive feeling in the person giving it. I love Ephesians 4:32 "And be kind to one another, tender hearted, forgiving each other, just as God in Christ also has forgiven you." I can do this simply by smiling.

20. What will I do to be calm? <u>Spend time outdoors.</u>

Being outdoors is the culmination of God's creation of nature. It is the ultimate environment meant for our enjoyment. When I'm outside I experience tranquility, serenity, and peace. I am able to let go or expel all feelings of stress, nervousness, and anxiety. I am reminded that God created all things perfectly and I am part of His creation. Being outdoors makes me feel like I belong to something larger then myself and I am calm.

The Test of Time demands answers to questions that result in a desirable outcome for those who are willing to dedicate time to find the answers. The Test of Time will change your life for the better if you take action and persevere. It answers the question of "What should I do with my time?"

Wouldn't it be great that at the end of each day you could say you are fulfilled, satisfied, content, peaceful, purposeful, loved, courageous, free, pleased, grateful, confident, accepted, delighted, happy, trusted, joyful, hopeful, inspired, kind and calm? This is what I strive for. This is what I desire.

If you are searching for answers to the following questions, the Bible is the greatest book ever written. In it God Himself speaks to you. It is a book of divine instruction offering comfort in sorrow, guidance in perplexity, advice for our problems, rebuke for our sins, and daily inspiration for our every need. The Bible alone truly answers the greatest questions that people of all ages have asked:

- Where have I come from?
- Where am I going?
- Why am I here?
- How can I know the truth?
- What should I do with my time?

For the Bible reveals the truth about God, explains the origin of man, points out the only way to salvation and eternal life, and explains the age-old problem of sin and suffering.

The great theme of the Bible is the Lord Jesus Christ and His work of redemption for mankind. The person and work of Jesus Christ are promised, prophesied, and pictured in the types and symbols of the Old Testament. In all of His truth and beauty, the Lord Jesus Christ is revealed in the Gospels;

and the full meanings of His life, His death, and His resurrection are explained in the Bible. His glorious coming again to earth in the future is unmistakably foretold in the book of Revelation. The great purpose of the written Word of God, the Bible, is to reveal the living Word of God, the Lord Jesus Christ.

God has given us the Bible in order that we might know Him and that we might do His will here on earth.

Therefore, devotional Bible study is the most important kind of Bible study. Devotional Bible study means reading and studying the Word of God in order that we may hear God's voice and that we may know how to do His will and to live a better Christian life.

The more you read the Bible, the more you will understand that in it God is revealing His way of salvation(a saving or being saved) to us from beginning to end.

Christians should know the Bible for many reasons, but the primary one is because God is its author.

The practical benefits for us may well be summarized under two headings: knowing and growing. The Bible proclaims the good news of the gospel that we might know God; it explains the will of God that all of us may grow spiritually before Him.

Scripture also reveals our place within God's program and answers crucial questions pertaining to our origin, purpose, and destiny. Because God has revealed His unchanging truths, the Christian faith provides real answers and guidance to every generation. Although we cannot grasp how individual events fit into God's program as stated in Eccl. 11:5: *"Just as you do not know the path of the wind and how bones are formed in the womb of the pregnant woman, so you do not know the activity of God who makes all things."* we can understand God's basic plan in order to come to know and serve Him. Few joys can compare with realizing our places in God's program and working to fulfill our destinies.

Now is your time to grow vigorously and thrive, by carving out precious time in your day to read and study the Bible, the Word of God, in order that you may find meaning, purpose and fulfillment in your life.

May God abundantly bless you as you place your trust in Him!

All my love and prayers that you may develop an intimate relationship with the Lord Jesus Christ by spending time with Him and His Word!

It's Time~Flourish Now —Grow vigorously and thrive!

Grow Vigorously & Thrive

- Be in constant communion with God, sharing and exchanging intimate thoughts and feelings.
- There are too many worldly distractions that turn my attention away from the beautiful moments that God has in store for me.
- The test of time is a real predictor of what I will do to make sure I spend time in a way that sets each day up for abundant success.
- By taking this Test of Time every morning, I set the day up to spend time on things that will be meaningful, give my life purpose and allow me to be fulfilled.
- If you are searching for answers to age-old questions, the Bible is the greatest book ever written that has every answer.
- For the Bible reveals the truth about God, explains the origin of man, points out the only way to salvation and eternal life, and explains the age-old problem of sin and suffering.

- God has given us the Bible in order that we might know Him and that we might do His will here on earth.
- The Bible proclaims the good news of the gospel that we might know God; it explains the will of God that all of us may grow spiritually before Him.
- Set aside some precious time in your day to read and study the Bible, the Word of God, in order that you may find meaning, purpose and fulfillment in your life.

ABOUT THE AUTHOR
Kristi Floersch

Kristi Floersch has a heart of compassion for people who have found themselves in a place of discontentment, who are overwhelmed, disinterested, fatigued, unengaged and spiritless and simply don't know what to do with their time.

She understands and cares about your wellbeing because she has been there and found the way out and wants the same for you. Her greatest desire is to help people find meaning, purpose and fulfillment with the time they've been given. She believes life is too short to be miserable. Kristi's name means, "Believer in Christ" and she is madly in love with Him because of the care, compassion and help He has provided to get her out of life's hard circumstances.

ABOUT THE AUTHOR

She believes that life is a short gift and it's time to flourish now and grow vigorously and thrive.

Kristi resides in Minnesota with her brilliant, witty and fun loving husband E.B. of 30 years. Together they have two adult children who are contributing beautifully to society in many generous and profound charitable ways. Kristi loves to water color paint and all things art. She also likes to spend time in her prayer room conversing with Jesus, reading books, snuggling babies and soft furry animals, connecting with people, and pursuing an active lifestyle. In July (the only month in MN that guarantees a few 80 degree days) you will find her soaking in summer sunshine in the land of 10,000 lakes with her family onboard a weekend pontoon ride to a local lakeside pizza .eatery dressed in nothing more than a cover up over a swimsuit wearing flip flops and enjoying "Macho Nacho's and an ice cold beverage. However, as you can tell by this book, her greatest passion is inspiring people to spend time in the Bible and in the presence of Jesus in order to design a life of meaning, purpose and fulfillment and to discover how to spend eternity with Him in heaven.

For more information visit www.FlourishNow.net